ABCD *Handbook*

A framework
for evaluating
community
development

by
Alan Barr &
Stuart Hashagen

COMMUNITY DEVELOPMENT FOUNDATION
• PUBLICATIONS •

Published in Great Britain by the
Community Development Foundation
60 Highbury Grove
London N5 2AG

Registered Charity Number 306130

First published in 2000
Reprinted in 2002

British Library Cataloguing-in-Publication Data
A record of this publication is available from the British Library

ISBN 1 901974 20 0

Cover design, text design and typesetting by Third Column, Twickenham

Printed in Great Britain by Elmtree Graphics , Colchester

Community Development Foundation

The Community Development Foundation (CDF) was set up in 1968. It pioneers, studies and disseminates new forms of community development.

CDF strengthens communities by ensuring the effective participation of people in determining the conditions which affect their lives. It does this through:

● providing support for community initiatives
● promoting best practice
● informing policy-makers at local, regional, national and international levels.

A leading authority on community development in the UK and mainland Europe, CDF is a non-departmental public body and is supported by the Active Community Unit of the Home Office. It receives substantial backing from local and central government, trusts and business.

CDF promotes community development through:

● local action projects
● conferences and seminars
● consultancies and training programmes
● research and evaluation services
● public policy analysis
● information services and web site
● publications.

Contents

Introduction ....*page 1*

Section **A**   **Achieving** Better Community Development ....*page 7*

Section **B**   Achieving **Better** Community Development ....*page 21*

Section **C**   Achieving Better **Community** Development...*page 47*

Section **D**   Achieving Better Community **Development**..*page 75*

Acknowledgements

We are grateful to the government departments that contributed to the funding of the ABCD programme: the Active Community Unit of the Home Office, the Voluntary Activity Unit of the Department of Health and Social Services in Northern Ireland, the Department of Social, Community and Family Affairs, in Ireland, the Scottish Executive Voluntary Issues Unit and the Scottish Executive Education Department.

Many people have been involved in the development of ABCD and have contributed ideas, experiences, criticisms and comments that have helped shape this handbook and other ABCD materials. Jacky Drysdale and Rod Purcell helped develop the original ABCD pack. They were joined by Sonya Murray, Mandy Wilson and Steve Brown in delivering the ABCD training programme. Graham Johnson originated the 'pyramid' form of ABCD. We thank them all for their contribution. We also drew many ideas and much inspiration from the enthusiasm with which so many participants in the training programme took up the ideas and ran with them. In particular we would like to thank the Amethyst Project, the community development staff of Brighton and Glasgow, Yorkshire Forward and East End Health Action for allowing us to draw on their experiences.

Introduction

abcd

Origins of ABCD.. *page 3*

What you will find in the handbook.. *page 4*

Related materials and resources.. *page 5*

Origins of ABCD

ABCD is a framework for understanding, planning, evaluating and learning from community development. It emphasises the participation of all stakeholders, especially communities themselves.

ABCD was developed by the Scottish Community Development Centre – a partnership between the Community Development Foundation and the University of Glasgow. It is based on work carried out by the Centre between 1994 and 1996. In 1996 the Centre published 'Learning for Change: community education and community development'. This study of the relationship between community education and community development in Scotland recommended, amongst other things, that there should be a clearer and more explicit framework within which both community education and community development could be understood, for the purpose of planning and evaluation. In 1996 the Centre undertook work, commissioned by the Northern Ireland DHSS Voluntary Activity Unit, to develop a set of indicators, and guidance on the evaluation of community development programmes. The development of the ABCD indicators was based on a framework of outcomes initially defined in 'Learning for Change', and informed by substantial consultation with practitioners and community activists in the community development field, including meetings in York, Glasgow, Dublin, Belfast, Derry/Londonderry and Enniskillen. It resulted in two publications:

● Monitoring and Evaluation of Community Development in Northern Ireland
● Measuring Community Development in Northern Ireland: a handbook for practitioners

These publications were launched at a conference in Belfast in 1996. Their contents were welcomed by a broad cross-section of community development funders, programme managers and community and voluntary organisations. However, there was a strong call for training and support to be provided, to help organisations develop and implement the evaluation system. Five government departments (the Active Community Unit of the Home Office, the Voluntary Issues Unit of the Scottish Executive, the Scottish Executive Education Department, the Northern Ireland DHSS Voluntary Action Unit and the Department of Social, Community and Family Affairs, Ireland) contributed to a common programme to provide such training. The Community Development Evaluation Skills Strategy, later renamed ABCD, got under way in April 1997.

The programme provided 26 five-day courses, backed by consultancy and networking support to participants, and an internet-based practice exchange. The course was free to participants, provided that they agreed to apply the model to their work and share their experience with others. Much of the practice experience drawn on in later sections of this handbook is an outcome of the readiness of participants to work in this way.

What you will find in the handbook

The handbook is divided into four main sections:

A describes ABCD, and explores issues in community development practice

B identifies ten core 'dimensions' of community development, describes these in detail, and provides a framework for evaluation through measures and indicators relating to strengthening communities

C draws on the framework in section B and explores, in detail, each of the key concepts of ABCD and how they can be used for better planning, managing, understanding, and learning from community development

D provides an illustration of the application of ABCD

Section A shows how achieving a coherent approach to community development can both strengthen communities and respond to the policy agenda in specific fields. It includes a critique of community development, but sets out a future direction. Refer to this section for a discussion of the nature of community development, and some of the issues that are addressed by ABCD.

Section B provides detail on each of the ten core dimensions of community development and shows how they can be divided into elements which are sufficiently specific to inform planning and evaluation. It offers a set of criteria on which the nature and level of development in communities can be judged and assessments of strengths and weaknesses made. It presents a menu as a stimulus – we encourage users to define their own criteria on the basis of the framework offered. Indeed it is good practice to find ways to encourage communities themselves to define and express the changes they need.

Section C discusses the key concepts of ABCD and suggests how they can be systematically applied to practice. It can aid understanding of how community development works: the relationship between the resources invested in it, the processes of change, the direct outputs or products of community development, and the wider outcomes it may lead to. It also suggests the stages that should be built into planning the activity – making sure all the key interests are involved, that there is clarity about what is expected from an initiative and that you are sure how you will know whether it is being achieved. It explicitly acknowledges the values that underpin community development.

Section D provides illustrative material that will be helpful in thinking through the ways ABCD can be used. It draws on experience to present the application of ABCD in a hypothetical community project.

Related materials and resources

This handbook should contain all the information most people will need to understand and apply the ABCD model. However, other materials are available. These include:

ABCD Trainers' Resource Pack

This provides additional material needed by trainers or senior managers wishing to implement ABCD as an agency wide approach. It contains the following materials:

— Suggested outline of one-day and two-day versions of the ABCD programme with trainers' notes.

— Standard set of 31 presentation panels which can be enlarged and reproduced as OHPs.

— Standard worksheets for use by participants in training programmes.

— Selected material drawn from the work of ABCD participants.

Available from CDF Publications (60 Highbury Grove, London N5 2AG, Tel: 020 7226 5375). £27.00 + £2.70 p&p. A4. 140pp approx. In ring-binder. Nov 2000.

Working with ABCD

This report is based on case studies of the ways ABCD has been applied, and draws together the issues for the future of community development which ABCD has identified.

Available from CDF Publications (60 Highbury Grove, London N5 2AG, Tel: 020 7226 5375). £14.95 + £1.50 p&p. Paperback. A4. 96pp approx. Oct 2000.

Summary of programme and findings

A short briefing which draws on the experience of the ABCD programme to identify the contribution that an understanding of community development can make to a range of public policy issues.

Available free from the Scottish Community Development Centre (Suite 329, Baltic Chambers, 50 Wellington Street, Glasgow G2 6HJ, Tel: 0141 248 1924) on receipt of a stamped addressed envelope.

Learning Evaluation and Planning (LEAP)

This is a quality improvement framework for community education developed, like ABCD, by the Scottish Community Development Centre. It shares the same model of community development and the same approach to change. Where ABCD focuses on outcomes – on what a developed community is like – LEAP is about process: how workers involved in community development activity can promote individual empowerment and build community capacity by adopting a planned and critical approach to practice.

Available from CDF Publications (60 Highbury Grove, London N5 2AG, Tel: 020 7226 5375). £15.00 + £1.50 p&p. Paperback. A4. Spiral bound. 900261 03 0.

SCDC on the Internet

The Scottish Community Development Centre maintains a web site, which includes information on ABCD and related activities, and can help signpost visitors to community projects, agencies and organisations that have applied the approach to their work. The address of the web site is **http://www.scdc.org.uk**

Achieving

Better

Community

Development

abcd

a1 **About ABCD**..*page 9*

a2 **Issues in community development**...*page 14*

a3 **Using ABCD**..*page 17*

About ABCD

Achieving better community development – ABCD – provides a framework for planning, evaluating and learning from community development interventions. It encourages those involved in community development – whether as funders, policymakers, managers, practitioners, volunteers or community members – to be clear about what they are trying to achieve, how they should go about it, and how they can change things in light of experience. It is a framework that is flexible enough to be applicable at policy, programme or project level, and sufficiently adaptable to reflect the priorities of community development activity at different times, in different places and with different people. This flexibility of application is counterbalanced by rigour in setting out what is, and what is not, community development.

ABCD is designed to be used by:

- members of community groups and organisations
- community workers employed by community organisations
- voluntary and public sector organisations
- workers in other fields who use community development approaches
- managers of community development programmes
- policy makers at all levels.

It focuses on what community development means and how you know whether it is taking place. Using ABCD helps clarify what community development work is trying to do, and provides information on which judgements can be made about progress. From these judgements, lessons for future work can be drawn. It is a tool for both planning and evaluation – and can also be used in other ways. It is left to organisations and workers to decide how best to use the framework to assist their work.

The approach provides an overall framework within which many other practice methods and techniques can be applied. For example, story-telling or planning for real can be used within ABCD. It emphasises the crucial importance of involving communities centrally in all aspects of community development work, and provides a tool for communities to be able to set an agenda for change, and to hold other partners to account.

The approach involves an understanding of:

- the *inputs* that can be brought to bear in community development activity
- the *process* of community empowerment, which lies at its heart
- the specific *outputs* of community development
- the *outcomes* or benefits to the quality of life in communities.

Within this framework it encourages communities themselves to identify the indicators and the information against which change can be identified.

This is a free-standing handbook that should provide enough information to allow managers, workers or community members to design planning and evaluation systems for all forms of community development. It presents the ABCD model of community development planning and evaluation, and sets out the knowledge and skills needed to apply the model to practice. Some users may need additional support and advice to help deal with issues from their own setting. Possible sources of such additional support are signposted in the Introduction.

It should be noted that other ways to evaluate community development are available. In particular, the established literature on participatory evaluation is helpful, and the various approaches to quality improvement in voluntary and community organisations complement ABCD. Many can be combined with the ABCD framework.

The key points

Before getting into the detail it may be helpful to set out the key ideas that underpin ABCD. Effective community development must engage in both planning and evaluation as central tools of good practice.

- Planning establishes a sense of direction and an understanding of who should do what.
- Evaluation is the basis on which we can learn from the process of change.

Planning and evaluation should be integral to community development

Community development work operates in a complex world. Communities vary enormously. Yet attention to planning and evaluation are always essential components of good practice. They are not optional; they are necessary elements of effective community development.

Communities of place may be villages, vibrant inner city neighbourhoods or run down outer city estates. People in communities may be bound by the ties of kinship or common culture, or divided among themselves. Community interest may range from a united opposition to an external threat – for example, proposals to build a road through a neighbourhood – to matters which relate only to the needs of particular groups – for example, the rights of travellers to public services. The practice methods adopted by community organisations and community development workers may also vary widely.

With this wide range of potential contexts, issues and methods it essential for community development to have a robust approach to planning and evaluation, in order that change can be identified, experience reflected on, and lessons learned. All those involved – funders, managers, workers and the community – need information on which they can base their understanding of what has happened, what has worked, what has not, what has changed, and why. It is this knowledge that enables practice to become more effective and efficient.

Evaluation is fundamental to empowerment

We argue that the core process of community development is the empowerment of communities, and explore this more fully in section C. High quality information is fundamental to the understanding and exercising of power. Evaluation is the means by which we can gain such information and understanding. In turn this enables us to learn how to tackle problems more effectively. Thus it follows, that if evaluation is an integral element of community development it is, by extension, an integral element of empowerment. If community development is to justify its role in promoting citizenship, social inclusion and learning through empowering people, it is crucial that it can identify and provide evidence about how empowerment has taken place, and how it has contributed to wider outcomes.

Evaluation is part of a learning organisation

A learning organisation is one that interacts with its environment, and is flexible, open and responsive to change. To be effective, community organisations themselves, the agencies that support their work, and the public, voluntary or private sector agencies that provide services to communities, should adopt the characteristics of learning organisations. The complexity of community development means that good information is needed as a base for learning. Thus evaluation of its work and impact is central to the nature of a learning organisation.

Community development has measurable outputs and outcomes

The history of community development is littered with unfortunate stereotypes. Those who accuse it of 'woolly-minded do-goodery' are complemented by those who think of it as the source of orchestrated and politically motivated challenge to the status quo. That these stereotypes persist is firm evidence that community development has largely failed to identify, own and communicate what it does and how it does it.

It is essential to be able to measure the outputs and outcomes of community development. ABCD brings together, analyses and codifies its components. ABCD presents an approach to evaluation, based on the principles of community development itself. It describes the processes of community empowerment, its outputs and outcomes, and their impact on the quality of life in communities. Such a framework is of value to agencies wishing to describe to others what their role in community development is and, equally importantly, what it is not. This can provide the evidence to allow judgements to be made about the value and impact of the work. Only on this basis will community development be recognised as an activity with an equivalent value to other strategies in regeneration and governance.

Community development must be participative – the community must be effective partners

The values of community development emphasise collaboration, community involvement and community-led agendas. Community development cannot therefore be properly evaluated by using externally imposed, goal-oriented and cost-based models. This is not to suggest that having clear goals, and considering the costs involved are unimportant. It is for the partners involved to agree these, and to consider the relationship between costs and benefits.

Community development is a process of change that necessarily involves many agents. Public sector agencies typically provide the policy environment, funding and resource base within which much community development operates. Statutory and voluntary organisations may provide various types of educational, organisational or administrative support to communities. Communities and their organisations make a major commitment of time, energy and local resources. If all these interests are necessary parties to community development they should all be party to its planning and evaluation, and to the learning of lessons it stimulates.

Models of evaluation based on externally designated performance goals do not meet the needs of the complex world of community development. They often assume causal links between action and effect, which demonstrates lack of understanding of the realities of how community development operates. They fail to promote an understanding of process and qualitative change. Economically based models of evaluation that are centrally concerned with relative costs and benefits are also of limited value in community development. Clearly funders have a right to know whether their resources have been wisely spent, and we would all have an interest in understanding how limited resources could be most effectively deployed, but models of evaluation which only attempt to match defined outputs to costs are unlikely to be effective for understanding community development. ABCD offers an alternative model, based on community development principles, which seeks to define evaluation as a learning tool, to understand change by capturing and reflecting on as much of the process as possible, and to focus on the outcomes, not just the outputs.

The ABCD approach is indicative, not prescriptive

Given that community development operates in the complex and variable environments described earlier, it follows that prescriptive models of evaluation are inappropriate. Issues and needs, directions for change, measures and indicators for understanding outputs and outcomes have to be identified on a case by case, place by place basis. Each community development activity, whether project, programme or policy, needs to engage its stakeholders in the process: we discuss this in detail later. We are not suggesting that community development is anything you want it to be. The case by case negotiation of evaluation design has to be based on a clear framework within which the key components of community development are specified. Programmes have to demonstrate how they will address the components of community development. ABCD contains a framework that suggests how this can be done.

Community development operates at policy, programme and project levels

Much of the history of community development has been based on projects: local, small-scale initiatives closely woven into the communities they serve. But as it has developed, community development has become part of the programmes of many agencies. By programmes, we mean a series of linked activities developed and managed by organisations to achieve defined aims. They may include grants programmes, anti-poverty initiatives or neighbourhood centre provision. Such programmes are often the product of wider policies that embrace community development principles. There are, for example, policies on the importance of community involvement in regeneration programmes, or in addressing inequalities in health. Recognising this reality, it is therefore not good enough simply to evaluate projects: they are only one of several links in the chain. We must also evaluate programmes and policies to understand whether and how they contribute to community development, how they relate to each other, how they articulate across institutional and organisational boundaries, and how they support or constrain action in communities.

Please note that in the remainder of this handbook we use the term 'initiative' to refer generically to project, programme and policy levels.

Evaluation and planning should be integrally linked

We have referred to the close relationship between evaluation and planning. ABCD argues that a disciplined approach to evaluation must be based on a disciplined approach to planning. This involves thinking from the start about what a programme is intended to do, how you will know whether it has done it, and how you will understand change. Similarly, proper planning must involve consideration of evaluation: how you will know whether your plans are having the desired effect. ABCD is thus of equal value to planning community development interventions as it is to evaluating them.

Issues in community development

Despite its long traditions, it is only in recent times that the value of community development to public policy has become generally acknowledged. Work over many years in some of our most marginal communities has produced outcomes of great value to those communities, but such work has either been ignored by the wider world or dismissed as being too vague or confrontational. Now the view is changing. In Britain and Ireland, many years of community development work have led to the emergence of a large number of community-led organisations. These vary widely in their size, role, approach and influence, but all:

● originate in a concern with community needs and issues

● have their purpose and direction decided by the community group which stands to benefit from the activities

● benefit a wider constituency.

Community groups and organisations are active in public affairs, complementing, challenging or collaborating with public, voluntary and business organisations. They are increasingly involved in networks of support and exchange, and are increasingly to be found influencing policy and strategy at local, authority-wide and national levels.

This development has been paralleled in the way service providers in many sectors have come to recognise the importance of engaging actively and creatively with communities. For example, in housing management many landlords have appointed tenant participation officers to support the development of community organisations in the properties for which they are responsible. Indeed, in Scotland policy has encouraged the formation of community based housing associations as an effective way to ensure housing provision meets community need.

Community development has now entered mainstream policy thinking in a new way. The origins of ABCD lie in Northern Ireland where, since 1996, community development has been written into public policy in health and social services. In England, successive rounds of the Single Regeneration Budget required more active attention to be given to ways of involving communities. The new Scottish Parliament created a Minister for Communities in 1999, and has several programmes that illustrate the importance being given to community development. In Ireland the community development Programme runs projects in rural and urban communities. These developments have been broadly welcomed, although concern has been expressed that the policies may be hard to implement in an environment where many organisations that formerly employed community work staff no longer do so. Other concerns are that the embedding of community development within public policy may lead to an expectation that it should respond to a government-set agenda, rather than to a community-led one. While there continues to be a lack of real clarity about what is meant by community development, such dangers will be seen to persist. A framework for planning and evaluating community development, recognised and supported by policymakers, funders, practitioners and communities, can help alleviate such fears. The ABCD model provides such a framework.

Effective community development work can build individual confidence and organisational capacity in communities, and this can complement other policy initiatives to achieve a better quality of life in communities and more effective solutions to problems in communities. Community development expresses the values of fairness, empowerment, opportunity, choice, participation, mutuality, reciprocity and continuous improvement. These are the ingredients of strong communities.

But these ideas do not belong solely to a particular institution or service. They are expressed by people who work in a wide range of fields. Some examples are:

Health: in which policy and practice to tackle health inequality, for example, embraces the need for social inclusion, recognises the importance of economic and social opportunity enhanced by learning and acknowledges that active citizenship contributes to personal and community health. The concept of 'social capital', which is entering health promotion, is closely related to the community development ideas of empowerment and community capacity.

Urban and rural regeneration: in which community involvement has long been recognised as a crucial component of good practice. The Joseph Rowntree Foundation programme 'Action on Estates' has brought together a wide range of research that has emphasised this factor, while CDF has produced a series of guidelines on good practice in developing regeneration proposals to take account of the community role. There has also been the debate on the idea of 'capacity building' in communities, to which community development has much to contribute.

Local government: where the policy agenda on modernising local government, the application of Best Value principles, the introduction of community planning, community learning plans and user participation in care services are all examples of a shift in role of local government towards more participatory forms of democracy and the adoption of community development. As the Joseph Rowntree Foundation report 'Starting to Modernise' stated: 'Developing a stronger relationship with its public is central to local government's future. Tackling many of the issues confronting local authorities requires the involvement and ideas of local people.'

This discussion shows that a concern with community development is inherent to a wide range of fields of activity that seek to contribute to a good quality of individual and community life. Parallel developments are taking place in housing, social care, community safety and many other fields. ABCD is relevant to any agency or worker employing community development approaches to promote social inclusion, lifelong learning or active citizenship.

Planning and evaluating community development: the issues

As part of the ABCD training programme we asked participants to identify their concerns about the way community development is viewed and evaluated. The issues discussed here are those identified through this process. They are factors which are generally thought to obstruct effective planning and evaluation of community development.

Inappropriate evaluation models

Funders, communities and community workers may all have differing expectations of community development. There is often a pressure from funders to evaluate all initiatives, but also a frustration among other stakeholders that the terms of evaluation have often not been properly negotiated between funders, programme managers, projects and the community. It is important that an evaluation framework is developed, based on the needs and perspectives of all the stakeholders in community development activities. What is unhelpful, and it is an issue frequently identified by managers and project leaders, is the plethora of evaluation frameworks imposed by different funding regimes. Many of these are not framed in a community development context, and for projects funded under several programmes, leaders may have to account for the same work in quite different ways. This is an unnecessary and unhelpful burden.

Lack of an agreed agenda

There is the problem of a mismatch between what projects actually do, and what funders want their grants to produce. While projects tend to emphasise the importance of the process of community development – engaging people in dialogue about community issues and responses – funders are often concerned solely with demonstrable impact and outcomes. This is, for example, a fundamental issue in community health work, in which outcomes have traditionally been measured at a whole population level, based on quantitative data on health outcomes or behavioural change. This approach is of little value in community project work, which is based on small populations and focuses largely on qualitative change.

The burden of evaluation

There are widely held concerns that projects receive tiny amounts of funding, yet are burdened with unrealistic expectations about what they might achieve, and criticised for not producing clear evidence of how their work impacts. They are sometimes asked for large amounts of monitoring information and experience such demands as a burdensome imposition. Thus evaluation is too often seen as a negative process, often associated with cuts in funding or closure of projects, too often done at the last minute, and too often seen just as a value-for-money exercise.

No clear understanding of community development

The challenge of concisely but completely defining community development has exercised workers and commentators for many years. A whole host of definitions and statements is available. Particular difficulty is caused in trying to distinguish between the terms community work, community development and capacity building – which some use virtually interchangeably, while others specify precisely. This lack of clarity, and the consequent failure to value the contribution community development makes, is a disservice to communities and to community development work.

Many of these issues can be addressed if participants give proper consideration to the way initiatives are to be planned and evaluated. ABCD provides a framework for such consideration, and the way it can be applied is set out in the next section.

Using ABCD

Evaluation as the key to empowerment, planning and good practice

The ABCD approach argues that evaluation is the key to effective practice, and that it should be conducted in accordance with the values and principles of community development itself. This means:

- working with communities to develop a shared view about what community development interventions are there to do

- deciding how the community and other partners are going to work towards realising that vision

- bringing in the resources the community has itself, or can access

- providing opportunities for community members to play a direct role in the process

- ensuring the community has ownership over the outcome.

ABCD recommends that all the stakeholders, including community organisations, should be involved in:

- planning change, which includes negotiating and agreeing the inputs (resources available to the work), the processes of learning and change, and the expected outputs and outcomes

- evaluating progress, which includes agreeing the indicators to be used, participating in data collection, participating in the choice of evaluators, and being involved in assessing the evidence, thus sharing in the learning and reflection on the process

- deciding on appropriate changes in policy and practice, based on the evidence from the evaluation.

In this way, ABCD promotes genuine partnership in evaluation and planning. With such an approach the different perspectives and expectations of stakeholders can expressed, clarified and acknowledged. Decisions can then be reached about the most critical issues for attention, how realistic objectives can be set and how progress will be recognised. With a clear and agreed agenda evaluation is much more likely to be viewed as a learning tool, rather than experienced as yet another pressure.

We noted above that a frequently raised issue is the lack of consensus about what community development actually is. Many claim to be doing it, but not all the work done in its name would meet the criteria normally thought to be part of it. Even within community development there is a wide range of definitions, each with its own emphasis. It is not the purpose of ABCD to try to develop yet another definition. However, certain assumptions are inherent in the ABCD approach. These are that:

- the idea of community includes communities of place, identity, and common interest
- community development is informed by, and based on a core set of values that shape the focus of its attention, inform the approach to practice and set out a vision
- community development is based on a cycle of change, involving inputs, processes, outputs and outcomes
- the nature of inputs, processes, outputs and outcomes can be analysed and measured
- planning and evaluating community development should be based on the same set of principles as community development itself.

ABCD is based on the broadly accepted values of community development endorsed by community development organisations, government departments and local government interests. These identify community development as an activity which confronts disadvantage, poverty and exclusion, and promotes values of active citizenship, learning and community participation. It is about change based on empowerment, leading to a better quality of community life. While community development activity is usually local, it needs to be located within broader policy frameworks that recognise its role and understand its contribution.

Applying the values of community development to planning and evaluation of the process leads to an approach with the following features. Community development programmes should:

Negotiate criteria and methods: Drawing on the experience, judgement and expectations of each of the stakeholders, criteria should be drawn from people's experience, and reflect the interests of all partners.

Avoid imposing indicators: Indicators need to be developed on a case by case basis to reflect the priorities of stakeholders in a given initiative. However, a framework within which indicators are suggested, such as that set out in section C, will be found useful as a trigger for local development or adaptation.

Provide a basis for learning: Learning is a key value in community development. For both communities and agencies, evaluation is the means by which the raw material for such learning can be assembled.

Contribute to community empowerment: Empowerment can only really take place when people have a full understanding of the environment and activities in which they are involved. Evaluation should provide such an understanding.

Help people acquire knowledge and skills for action: Evaluation provides insight into why certain things worked, while others did not; it provides a basis on which participants can review their actions and the responses of others, and leads to a consideration of how things might now be done better. Evaluation should thus inform both task goals and process goals – what people want to achieve and how.

Emphasise qualitative factors: Much formal evaluation focuses only on quantifiable evidence. Because community development emphasises both process and outcome, and perception and experience of change, qualitative evidence is crucial to a proper understanding. It is a central challenge for community development to establish the validity of qualitative factors and to develop more effective ways to assess change. By adopting such a stance, ABCD goes some way in setting the terms of this challenge.

Encourage communities to participate in choosing evaluators: Decisions about who is involved in evaluation and in what capacity are crucial. ABCD proposes a model of planning and evaluation that is inclusive, involving all stakeholders in the process. It follows that approaches to evaluation based solely on the deployment of external specialists are not consistent with ABCD. However, there may be certain instances where there are sound reasons for deploying specialists, and in such circumstances the community should be engaged in the drafting of briefs and in selection.

Engage community evaluators: As community development seeks to engage community members in community affairs, it follows that the evaluation of community development contains opportunities for employing community members to gather and interpret information. This is a particular opportunity for large, funded regeneration initiatives. Such initiatives increase the opportunities available to local people. They can work alongside others to evaluate the performance of partners in meeting agreed goals.

Consider the project, programme and policy levels: As we proposed earlier, community development typically operates at project, programme and policy levels. Each should therefore be evaluated.

Achieving
Better
Community
Development

b1 The dimensions of community development...........................*page 23*

b2 Personal empowerment: a learning community.......................*page 27*

b3 Positive action: a fair and just community...............................*page 29*

b4 Community organisation: an active community........................*page 31*

b5 Participation and involvement: an influential
community..*page 34*

b6 A shared wealth: community economic development..........*page 36*

b7 A caring community: social and service development.........*page 39*

b8 A safe and healthy community: community
environmental action..*page 41*

b9 A creative community: arts and cultural
development..*page 43*

b10 A citizens' community: governance and development........*page 44*

b11 The strengthened community..*page 46*

The dimensions of community development

The diagram below provides an analysis of community development that breaks it down into a series of dimensions, each of which can be examined in detail. That is the purpose of this section of the handbook. For each dimension we:

- describe what it is and why it is important

- break it down into its component parts – which we call 'elements'

- suggest some techniques that you could use to understand the way in which your programme contributes to change.

There are two sets of dimensions: those concerned with community empowerment (B2 to B5), and those concerned with the quality of community life (B6 to B10). The relationship between the dimensions of community development can be shown diagrammatically:

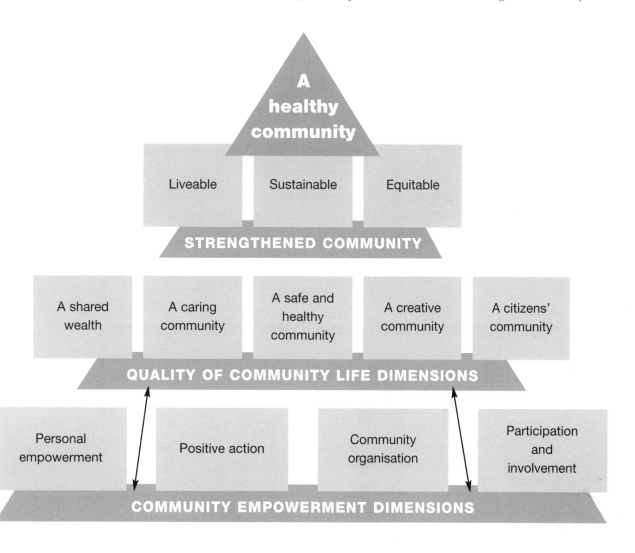

Achieving **Better** Community Development

Community empowerment dimensions

At the heart of the ABCD approach is the idea of community empowerment. We describe it as a 'core purpose' of community development, the other core purpose being to gain improvement in the quality of community life. The general concept of community empowerment can be understood in a variety of ways.

- As a process which utilises inputs to attain intended outputs and outcomes.

- As the role of community workers and others who support the development of individuals and groups in communities, building up the strength of the community to act effectively on its needs.

- As the actions of communities, which leads to their exercising more influence over the affairs that affect them, and acting effectively in their own interests.

- As an outcome: an empowered community has identifiable, measurable characteristics.

It is particularly important to recognise that community empowerment is both a process and a product, and that it is the means by which wider changes of benefit to communities are realised. It is also essential to understand that community empowerment, and each of its dimensions, must be built in to the planning and evaluation of all community development activity. This is a central message of ABCD.

The four community empowerment dimensions are set out below, describing each as a process and as an outcome.

Community empowerment dimensions

Process	Outcome
Personal empowerment	A learning community
Positive action	A fair and just community
Community organising and volunteer support	An active and organised community
Participation and involvement	An influential community

The quality of community life dimensions

Our earlier discussion described community empowerment as being at the heart of community development, and we go to some lengths in the ABCD approach to specify what this means, why it is important, how it might be achieved, and how change can be measured. Yet the motivation for most, if not all, community development activity is to achieve change which addresses needs and issues in communities. Such changes might be material – for example a welfare benefits campaign to increase uptake of a particular benefit, they might be environmental – as with a local planning group to design traffic calming measures, or they could be social – perhaps a protest against the threatened closure of a cottage hospital. Indeed, many changes sought by communities may not fit readily

24 [CDF] Achieving Better Community Development: *ABCD Handbook*

into the sectors of public administration. For example, local action on dampness in social housing may be seen as a housing matter, a health matter, a poverty matter or an environmental/energy conservation matter.

It is in the area of quality of life that the 'bottom-up' meets the 'top-down'. Many areas of practice now have a community aspect, in which it is a matter of policy to work in a way that engages, involves and empowers communities. So, in the examples given above, a welfare rights advisor might be involved in assisting a benefits campaign, traffic planners could be involved in the traffic calming activity, and a campaign against a hospital closure might enjoy the advice of health visitors working in the community. For the staff involved, these issues can be challenging, but the crucial point is that change takes place where action that is inspired and led by a community meets a policy or service driven from above.

It is equally important to recognise that not all changes that bring benefit to the quality of life in communities can legitimately be claimed as community development outcomes. The inward investment that resulted in the creation of new jobs by Nissan in the employment desert of Sunderland, or the effects on one-parent families of the introduction of the working families tax credit are undeniably gains to the potential quality of life in communities. But they can hardly be ascribed to community development since those communities were not active in identifying need and lobbying for change. So, from a community development perspective it is important to see whether quality of life outcomes relate to the process of community development.

As with the community empowerment dimensions, the quality of life dimensions encapsulate the idea of process as well as the idea of outcome. They are:

Process	Outcome
Community economic development	A shared wealth
Social and service development	A caring community
Community environmental action	A safe and healthy community
Community arts and cultural development	A creative community
Governance and development	A citizens' community

We cannot be prescriptive about defining quality of life outcomes, as the desired outcomes will be identified in the context of local action. It is not possible to capture the detail of all possibilities. These notes therefore only offer general guidance. We would not expect all community development activities to address all the quality of life outcome dimensions, although we would encourage them to recognise the importance of the knock-on effect of one on another. For example, community health work is widely recognised as an important route thorough which women are brought into participation in wider community affairs, while community arts work can be invaluable in bringing different perspectives to the understanding of many community issues.

Working with the dimensions

It is important to note several points about these dimensions and the way they are described.

Certain of the dimensions and elements are essential to community development: by this we mean that any initiative that is not addressing each of them is not a community development initiative. All the community empowerment dimensions are critical and non-negotiable. Each is of value in its own right, but it is the combination of all four that constitutes community development. All community development programmes should be able to demonstrate how they understand each dimension, how they use it to understand the level and profile of empowerment in their community, how they are working to advance it, and how they will know what changes.

Within the community empowerment dimensions we provide lists of elements. We consider some to be so important that all community development programmes should include them. Others are listed as a menu from which you may select relevant items. Also, do remember that you may develop your own elements and indicators to reflect your programme's particular plans and priorities.

For the quality of community life dimensions, we do not mark any of the elements as critical or non-negotiable. This is because the quality of life issues that programmes work on vary widely. For example, a community economic development programme would not necessarily expect to produce outcomes in the area of culture and celebration. However, it is likely that most programmes will need to do much more work, involving their stakeholders, to identify the expected outcomes. These may well be quite specific to the time and place of each programme. Our tables are thus only a rough guide and should be treated as such.

For each set of elements we also provide a list of the type of evidence that can be sought to indicate what change is taking place. It is particularly important to recognise that it is possible to find ways to measure even the most apparently intangible aspect of community development. It is also important to recognise that evidence may relate to people themselves, in community relationships and structures, and in agency policies and services. The more that evidence can be sought from a range of sources, the more robust the conclusions are likely to be.

We now move to a discussion of each of the community empowerment dimensions, followed by a similar discussion of the quality of community life dimensions. We describe each, and explain how it relates to the values and principles of community development. We then list some core components of each and suggest ways in which they might be measured. The elements that should be considered essential to community development are highlighted in bold.

When applying the framework to your own initiative you should remember that activity in all the dimensions of community empowerment is critical to community development, so all dimensions should all be considered and included. In the quality of community life dimensions you should recognise the links between the categories: for example an environmental change may well have an economic outcome, and you should also check how the quality of life changes relate to the process of community empowerment. The quality of community life dimensions are indicative. We would encourage initiatives to develop their own indicators on the basis of the framework we offer.

We do not provide detailed guidance on how information on each indicator might be gathered, as this will vary according to the circumstances of each initiative. There is a discussion of information gathering in sections B7 and B8 and you should refer to these sections for guidance.

Personal empowerment:
a learning community

By personal empowerment we mean the processes through which individuals and groups of people gain the knowledge, skill and confidence they need to be able to take action on matters that concern them. It is the fundamental process of community development. Yet there are many obstacles to personal empowerment.

- Many excluded people live their lives in a dependent or alienated way and do not perceive the possibility of change.

- Others may believe change is possible, but that external pressures are so great that there is no point in trying to change things.

- Some would think change possible but would leave it to others, or feel they lack the skills or confidence to take action themselves.

- Others may fear that by taking action they would be laying themselves open to sanctions or punishment by more powerful forces.

These forces all conspire against disadvantaged or excluded communities acting in their own interests. It is for this reason that community development, and much of its theory, starts with the question of how to empower people to take action.

The idea of personal empowerment responds to several of the values described in section B2. Lack of self-esteem, lack of leverage and fear of reprisal are all forces that sustain division in society, and are all obstacles to active citizenship and change. Acting on this exclusion by helping people to understand these forces and recognise that change may be possible and worthwhile is fundamental to the idea of empowerment and participation. In this approach experience is used as a route to learning.

Breaking the general idea of personal empowerment into component 'elements' which are sufficiently concrete to use as a basis for planning, action and evaluation leads to the following framework.

Elements of a learning community

- Are people confident that things can be changed for the better?
- Do people have the skills they need – to collect and use information, to negotiate, to organise, to plan action, to manage budgets?
- Do people have the knowledge they need – of community issues, needs and resources, of how the decisions that affect them are made, of the way decisions can be influenced?
- Is leadership developed in the community strong and accountable?
- Do people understand how to use power for community benefit?

— What opportunities are there to help people learn from their experience of action? Do any of these lead to qualifications that can be used elsewhere?

Possible measures

In people

— Are people confident that change is possible and worthwhile?

— What knowledge and skills have been developed by people through being involved in community activity?

— How have these skills been applied to action in the community?

— What qualifications have people gained?

In the community

— Are people active in community affairs generally?

— Are people active in community groups and community organisations?

— Are community organisations run in an open and democratic way?

— How do community organisations use their influence to create change?

In local services

— What formal and informal opportunities are provided by schools, colleges and other educators to help people think about and learn from their experiences?

— Do any of these opportunities lead to or provide recognised qualifications?

— Do agencies such as schools and government offices try to identify and remove any obstacles to people making their views known?

— Do agencies positively encourage people to take part in planning and carrying out their work?

In policies

— Do the agencies in the community have policies which recognise the right of people to participate, and which encourage this by removing obstacles and encouraging access?

— Do agencies have policies which actively seek to give their users more power in planning, monitoring and developing their work?

— What systems are in place to ensure such policies are being put into effect?

Positive action:
a fair and just community

We have adopted the term 'positive action' to convey the sum of meanings included in the concepts of equal opportunity, social justice, social inclusion and anti-discriminatory practice. The idea of positive action is fundamental to community development because the source of obstacles to community change and progress lies in imbalances in access to power, to being heard, or in active discrimination against certain groups. One basic value of community development is that no one group should gain at the cost of others, another is that change builds on an acceptance and understanding of others. Exclusion on the grounds of disability or race is widely discussed. It is also important to recognise that people may be excluded by poverty, culture or the actions of public policy. Exclusion may also operate within communities. Some community leaders may represent their constituencies without any form of accountability, or may try to maintain one set of values against another. ('I speak for the respectable members of this community...') The key to understanding positive action is to recognise systems of power, dominance and sub-servience, and to seek to challenge or dismantle them.

Elements of a fair and just community

— Do partners accept that the principles of social justice and collective support should underpin community activity?

— Is action in the community based on social justice and opportunity for all?

— Are the needs of excluded individuals and groups understood?

— Do projects and programmes consider everybody's needs and record any discrimination?

— Is cultural heritage and identity recognised and affirmed?

— Are people free to celebrate their identity and culture?

— Do projects and programmes have equal opportunity policies?

— Does their practice promote equal opportunities?

Possible measures

In people

— Do minority group members feel accepted and valued?

— Do they feel that they can express their culture?

In the community

— Do minority community members participate in community groups and their activities?

— Do community organisations have equal opportunity policies?

— What community organisations are involved in work on culture and identity?

— What activities do they encourage?

In local services

— Are the needs of women, disabled people, minority ethnic, cultural and religious groups investigated and recorded?

— What action is taken to ensure all minorities receive services?

— Have services changed to meet the needs of minority groups?

— Are there structures to support the involvement of minority group members?

In policies

— Do agencies in the community have equal opportunity policies?

— Are these policies relevant to needs in the community?

— Is the implementation of the policies monitored, and how is the evidence used?

— Do agencies understand the values of community development?

Community organisation:
an active community

This encompasses general activity in the community, the range, quality and effectiveness of community based groups and organisations, and the nature and quality of their relationships with each other and the wider world.

A central purpose of community development is to strengthen the range and quality of organisation in communities. This works at several levels.

The first may be termed informal social care and networking. This includes getting to know other people, keeping an eye on neighbours' homes while they are away, perhaps helping older people with shopping or gardening, and lending tools or books.

The next level is where these activities become a little more organised – involving baby-sitting circles, parent and toddler groups, or neighbourhood watch schemes.

Then there are groups that exist to identify and represent community needs and issues. These may include school boards, community councils, neighbourhood forums and tenants associations.

More formal community-led organisations may emerge. They may employ staff, have buildings or other assets, and offer a range of services or activities in communities. Examples include community-based housing associations, development trusts and independent living centres.

At a broader level, there are organisations within the community sector that serve to represent common interests or provide services.

The role of community development in strengthening community organisation has several elements.

Elements of an active community

— Are local people active in community organisations?

— Do local people use the services provided by community organisations?

— Are there support and exchange networks in the community?

— Are people active in the way services, such as schools, are run?

— Do community groups know about community needs, problems, resources and assets?

— Do community groups run services and activities?

— Are community organisations open, democratic and accountable?

— Are there support and exchange networks between community organisations?

— Are community organisations involved with other local bodies?

— Do community organisations have relationships with people elsewhere working on the same problems?

— Does the community own and manage its own organisations?

— Does the community own resources and assets which support long-term action?

Possible measures

In people

— How many people are involved in the work of community organisations?

— How much time do they give?

— What knowledge and skills do they bring in?

— Do people involve themselves in local services, for example schools or leisure centres?

In the community

— What services and facilities are provided by community organisations?

— How often are they used?

— How many people use them?

— Do the services meet people's needs?

— Are the services valued by users?

— What informal networks exist in the community?

— What do these networks do?

— How are they used?

— How do community organisations find out what needs there are?

— What information shows that they have a good understanding of needs?

— How many services and facilities do community organisations run?

— What do these services and facilities do?

— Do community organisations provide information about their activities and plans?

— Are their meetings well publicised and open?

— In what ways do community organisations link to others and work with them?

— In what ways do these links help the organisations involved?

— In what ways are community organisations involved in other local bodies (for example in planning boards, area committees, policy development groups, partnerships)?

— In what ways are community organisations involved in collaboration or alliances with other groups at regional, national or international levels?

— What degree of influence and control does the community have over service agencies?

In local services

— Are local service agencies aware of the services provided by the community?

— Do they refer people to them?

— Do they provide other sorts of help?

— Are services such as schools open to parental and community involvement?

— How do they encourage such involvement?

— What help and resources are provided to help community organisations run services and facilities?

— What support is provided to help community organisations be more effective (for example community work, training, financial advice)

— Is this support relevant and valued?

— What grants schemes exist to support community organisations?

— Are they operated fairly and openly?

— What mechanisms are in place to involve the community or service users in planning and delivering services or in planning investment?

— What public buildings and equipment are available for community organisations to use?

In policies

— Do local authorities' and other organisations' policies refer to the importance of an active and involved community?

— Do they set out ways to encourage such activity?

— Do they set out ways to ensure it is being encouraged?

— Is there political will to support community organisation?

Participation and involvement:
an influential community

The crux of the ABCD approach lies here. We have proposed that community development has the two main purposes of community empowerment and improving the quality of community life. It is through participation and influence that the empowered community interacts with the outside world to achieve change. Therefore, in planning and evaluating community development, it is crucial to understand the relationships between communities and political, administrative and service-providing systems, to look at how communities go about working for change, and to consider obstacles and opportunities. Agencies that are committed to community development must also consider how they go about maximising the opportunities for communities to participate and have influence over the way they work.

Elements of an influential community

— Are there strong and democratic organisations in the community?

— Are community organisations effective in influencing the policy of agencies working in the community?

— Are community organisations effective in influencing the practice of agencies working in the community?

— Does the community control its own assets and services?

Possible measures

In people

— Do people generally feel confident and assertive about getting things done?

— Do they demonstrate confidence?

In the community

— What groups and organisations are active in the community?

— How active are local people in the work of groups and organisations?

— Are they constituted to be open and democratic in the way they work?

— Are community organisations represented on planning and policy making bodies?

— What is their influence on decisions?

— What services or facilities are managed by the community?

— What services or facilities are owned by the community?

In local services

— In what ways are the views of the community sought?

— Are the views expressed acted upon?

— What is the attitude of service providers to the community?

— What services are managed and delivered with direct community involvement?

In policies

— Do policies specify the importance of community involvement in decision making?

— Do they set out the reasons for community involvement?

— Do they establish targets and performance measures?

A shared wealth:
community economic development

There has been a long tradition of community economic development in both Britain and Ireland. From the mid 1970s community businesses were being established, while in the 1980s much of the force of regeneration was directed to creating jobs and training for those excluded from the labour market. This thinking has persisted, and more recently has linked up with the other arm of community economic activity – anti-poverty and welfare rights campaigning. There are now many sorts of community organisation that form an important part of their local economies – providing services, providing alternatives or encouraging access. Examples include:

● development trusts

● community businesses

● credit unions

● local exchange trading schemes (LETS)

● debt counselling and money advice services

● community chests

● community based housing associations.

We take the view that these activities all contribute to the community economy. They all seek to increase incomes, to reduce costs, or to increase the number and range of assets within community control. Other initiatives, such as house insulation or community transport schemes, may have environmental or social benefit, but also serve to reduce costs. Senior citizens' lunch clubs are another example. All such initiatives have the potential to become community enterprises. Community economic development can be related to those values of community development that combat poverty and exclusion, and which seek to reduce inequality and division.

Elements of community economic development

— Increasing income to individuals, families and groups: are people receiving all the benefits to which they are entitled?

— Developing skills and competence within the labour market: are there activities to increase local people's chances getting jobs?

— Creating or changing job opportunities: does the community influence the investment decisions of businesses or economic development agencies?

— Do people have fair and equal access to jobs?

— Are costs for individuals, families and groups reducing?

— Is the community attracting external funds into projects, initiatives and facilities, thus reducing dependence on the formal economy?

— Does the community add value to such investment through unpaid voluntary activity?

— Do local organisations trade goods and services in other communities?

— What is the quality and nature of public services in the economic sphere: jobcentres, employment services, economic development agencies?

— Are there activities to retain and recycle wealth in the community, for example credit unions or local co-operatives?

— Are there activities designed to reduce the costs of living in the community?

— Are goods and services being sourced and supplied within the community?

— Are there business and enterprise activities controlled by the community that increase community assets (for example, community businesses or co-operatives)?

— Is there access to good quality financial services (for example, credit, banking and debt advice)?

Possible measures

In people

— How many community members are employed in community-led enterprises?

— What is the nature of their work?

— What are the wage levels and security of the jobs?

— Are people receiving all the welfare benefits to which they are entitled?

— Is the value of unpaid voluntary activity recognised in programmes for the community?

In the community

— How many community businesses, enterprises and other economic initiatives are there in the community (for example, credit unions, food co-ops and LETS schemes)?

— What other economic assets are owned by the community?

— Are there community-led schemes designed to keep wealth in the community (for example, community transport schemes)?

— Is the community successful in attracting external funds for projects and activities?

— Does the community produce goods or services?

— Does it trade goods and services with other communities?

In local services

— Have investment, recruitment or other business decisions been influenced by the community?

— If so, in what ways?

— Are there any arrangements for businesses to consult with the community?

— Are there any agency agreements or contracts through which community organisations deliver services?

— Do public agencies provide information and encouragement for people to claim all their benefits entitlement?

— What initiatives are there to help train and place community members in available work?

— How well do the goods and services provided meet community needs?

In policies

— Are there economic policies designed to encourage investment into the community?

— Are there policies designed to reduce the costs of living in the community (for example, housing insulation schemes)?

A caring community:
social and service development

One of the most important characteristics of a strong community is the nature of the support and care it offers its members. We noted in our discussion of community activity and organisation that there are many levels of activity in communities that support members. It is also the case that much of the focus of participation and influence is on the nature and quality of social service provision. In this dimension we are essentially looking at the nature and extent of those services that support and sustain people's life in communities. These are wide ranging and include:

● information and communication services

● education services: formal, informal and community

● health services

● caring services: for particular groups as well as the community as a whole

● advice and legal services

● shopping and commercial services.

While many such services are provided by local authorities this is not always the case. We are also interested in the services provided by commercial organisations, voluntary organisations and communities themselves.

Elements of a caring community

For each of these areas the community development questions are:

— What is the extent and quality of the service?

— How does it relate to local needs and issues?

— How does it involve community members in planning, delivery and development?

— Is the service available, accessible and responsive?

Possible measures

In people

— To what extent do community members participate in planning or providing services or in encouraging other organisations to do so?

In the community

— Is the community itself active in providing services in this area?

— If so, in what ways?

— What local action, campaigns or pressure is there on social development issues?

In local services

— Do local services provide opportunities and support to people who need it (for example, pre-school children, carers, older people, people with mental illness, people with learning difficulties)?

— If so, in what ways?

— Are the public services responsive to the views of users and of the community as a whole?

— If so, in what ways?

In policies

— To what extent do policies encourage open access, user feedback, local dialogue, participation and influence?

A safe and healthy community:
community environmental action

The stimulus for much community action has been a real or perceived threat to the health or safety of people living in communities. It is important to be aware that poor neighbourhoods are not just where poor people happen to live. They are almost invariably the least safe, least healthy, least stimulating environments, and the motivation to deal with these fears and dangers is the motivation behind everything from neighbourhood watch schemes, through protests against industrial pollution, to running voluntary after-school care schemes.

Elements of a safe and healthy community are wide ranging, but include the following:

● housing/insulation

● safe pedestrian routes

● open spaces

● safe play

● waste and pollution control

● low energy use

● sharing and recycling schemes

● transport

● community safety.

Elements of a safe and healthy community

— Are people generally satisfied with the environment of the community?

— Are people generally satisfied that the community is a healthy place to live?

— Are people generally satisfied with public transport services and provision for cycling and walking?

— Are people encouraged to recycle and re-use?

Possible measures

In people

— To what extent are community members aware of environmental issues and action?

In the community?

— Are there local recycling and refurbishment schemes?

In local services

— Are there appropriate waste management programmes?

— To what extent is there appropriate land reclamation and land use?

— What is the extent of air and ground pollution?

— What proportion of housing is properly insulated?

— What is the quality, frequency and cost of public transport?

— Are there any traffic management schemes to respond to community problems?

— Have cycle and pedestrian routes been provided as an alternative to car transport?

In policies

— To what extent do policies encourage open access, user feedback, local dialogue, participation and influence?

A creative community:
arts and cultural development

The bonds that build communities are as much about shared experience, celebration and culture as about economics, environment or services. All traditional cultures and communities have shared religious or other celebrations to mark the change in seasons, historical events or the religious calendar. Arts and drama are used, and can become a valuable method of helping communities identify and express issues and needs. The nature, variety and significance given to this is therefore an important part of community development and of the quality of community life. We take a broad view of the notion of a 'creative community' and include within it all forms of festivals, arts, sports and spiritual activity.

Elements of a creative community

— Sense of history and identity.

— Celebration of cultures.

— Participation in sport and recreation.

— Artistic expression – leading to personal and community development.

— Freedom of cultural and religious expression.

Possible measures

In people

— Do people feel connected to community and tradition?

— Do people value this connection?

In the community

— Are different cultures recognised, valued and celebrated?

In local services

— Are there accessible and responsive services to encourage participation in sport, recreation and arts?

In policies

— Do relevant policies recognise the importance of creativity and celebration and build them into services?

A citizens' community:
governance and development

Throughout ABCD we argue that there is no point to community development unless change is involved. The emphasis of the fourth dimension of community empowerment is precisely this: how communities can develop the capacity to influence change effectively. However, as well as being a process of empowerment, the context of political expression is an important component of the quality of community life. Although we may all live in a democracy with policy making and policy being a product of a recognised political process, the way that is experienced will vary widely. Some government activities will go much further than others in engaging the public in debating and developing policy, and the same is true of local government, non-elected boards and, indeed, voluntary organisations. As we know, community development emphasises the values of openness, dialogue, inclusion and participation, and the quality of community life is enhanced where these values are reflected.

Elements of a citizens' community

— Community engagement with elected representatives is encouraged.

— Knowledge and understanding of democratic procedures and how to influence them is encouraged.

— Direct community participation in decision making is supported.

— Community control of services and facilities is encouraged where the community wishes.

— Community organisations are encouraged to develop open, democratic, inclusive constitutions.

— Individuals are encouraged to participate effectively in organisations.

Possible measures

In people

— Do people make effective use of elected representatives?

— Is there evidence of enhanced personal and community capacity for change?

In the community

— Are there self-confident communities with greater investment in their futures?

— Is there strong community leadership?

— Are community organisations accountable, equitable and broadly based?

In local services

— Are elected representatives accountable and better engaged with their electorate?

— Are there strong foundations for community partnerships?

— Is there evidence of local and community influence?

In policies

— Are policies responsive to need?

— Are outcomes sustainable and equitable?

The strengthened community

As we have proposed throughout this handbook, community development is a process of empowering communities, leading to a more satisfactory quality of community life. We have broken down what we mean by empowerment, and we have also spelt out the dimensions of the quality of community life. Another central message has been the importance of values, and we have discussed the core values on which community development is built. We think it is important to be able to bring together these values, along with the process of empowerment and the idea of the quality of community life, into three overall ideas:

Sustainability: where there is a stable social, economic, physical and cultural infrastructure that has a lasting capacity to meet people's needs and promote community well-being.

Liveability: where people are satisfied and comfortable with their life circumstances: where and how they work, rest and play.

Equity: how fairly and justly people are treated in employment, housing and access to services.

If we were to provide a single, overall idea, we would suggest that community development is ultimately about the creation of healthy communities, following the World Health Organisation definition of health as 'a state of complete physical, mental and social well-being and not merely the absence of disease or infirmity'. We consider that all public policy, and not only community development, should reflect these ideas, and direct resources and effort to their attainment. Community development has a particular role to play – as described throughout this handbook.

We have not developed elements or indicators specific to these ideas, because if initiatives achieve progress in all the other dimensions and elements described, they will be achieving progress in creating sustainability, liveability and equitability. We suggest that these concepts are used as a framework for checking and discussing the proposed or actual outcomes of a community development activity. For this purpose, we can pose general questions, such as:

- can people meet their basic needs for food, shelter and clothing?
- do people have the opportunity for fulfilling work and leisure?
- can people express themselves and celebrate their identity?
- are people in control of their lives?
- are people safe and secure?
- do people enjoy good relations with others in the community?
- do people get justice and fair treatment?
- do people have equal access to the services they need?
- do public and private services provide equality of opportunity and equality of treatment?

Achieving
Better
Community
Development

c1 Stages in community development...*page 49*

c2 Values in community development...*page 52*

c3 Inputs, processes, outputs and outcomes...................................*page 55*

c4 The ABCD model...*page 60*

c5 Stakeholders...*page 63*

c6 Vision..*page 66*

c7 Dimensions, elements and indicators...*page 68*

c8 Getting information...*page 70*

c9 Assessing evidence, drawing conclusions,
learning lessons...*page 74*

Stages in community development

In this section we turn to thinking through how community development programmes can be planned, implemented and evaluated using the ABCD framework. This can be thought of as a process with nine steps. These are set out in sections C2 to C9 and can be summarised below:

Step 1: Understanding community development values and principles (C2)

Community development is based on a clear set of values and principles that define where and how it works, and distinguish it from other types of activity in communities. The first step is to appreciate the core values and their implications in relation to the particular context of practice

Step 2: Exploring the key components of community development (C3)

To carry out community development the people involved must have a clear idea of the resources they have at their disposal, the way these resources can be enhanced and directed towards change, and a recognition of what sort of change is needed. This means that the ideas of input, process, output and outcome, and the relationships between them, should be explored and understood.

Step 3: Understanding the ABCD model (C4)

The ABCD model is set out as a diagram. It identifies the need to consider inputs, processes, outputs and outcomes and expresses the relationship between the values and context of community development practice. In doing so it reflects the key purposes of community development – community empowerment and improving the quality of community life. The third step is to understand the model.

Step 4: Identifying and working with stakeholders (C5)

Stakeholders are the people or organisations with an interest in an activity and the capacity to influence its direction and outcome. In community development the key stakeholder is the community itself, but many other stakeholders must be considered and engaged if the outcome is to meet community needs. It is thus crucial to consider, as step four, who is involved, what they have to contribute, what they expect to get out of the process, and whether they are likely to be constructive or obstructive. Community development approaches are not always understood by all the stakeholders. It is important to be able to explain and explore the value of the approach, and some of the key ideas are set out in section C5.

Step 5: Setting the vision and defining the outcomes(C6)

This means involving the stakeholders in negotiating what the initiative is trying to achieve, and how it will work towards it. It is vital that the overall direction and purpose of activity is clear before more specific decisions about the resources and methods of intervention are agreed. This way the emphasis is placed on a needs-led approach. The needs and issues felt and expressed by the community are the crucial factor. Reaching a shared vision is essential but it must be translated into more specific outcome statements against which performance can be assessed. These are the tasks for step 5.

Step 6: Dimensions, elements and indicators (C7)

This step is at the heart of designing a working framework for planning, doing, and learning from community development activity. It involves defining how an initiative intends to empower communities and enhance the quality of community life by defining and agreeing the key dimensions, elements, measures and indicators which will be required. These have been discussed in detail in section B.

Step 7: Delivering change (C8)

Once you have established which dimensions and elements identify the character of the work needed to achieve your preferred outcome, it is then essential to specify the necessary inputs, who will provide them, the work methods you will use and the outputs of that work. Step 7 focuses attention on the practical tasks involved and the resources needed to undertake them.

Step 8: Collecting information and measuring change (C9)

Once it is clear what an initiative is trying to achieve, the next step is to establish what information is needed, how and when it will be collected, and how you will confirm whether and how change is taking place. These issues are focus of step 7.

Step 9: Learning from change (C10)

We have said that evaluation is primarily about learning from experience and doing things better. In C9 we look at the final step, how the information gathered about community development can be used to identify areas for attention and to celebrate achievement.

An overview – the community development cycle in brief

From the outset, it is important to stress that community development is a cyclical and continuous activity. Hence you are likely to need to return to the key stages several times during the lifetime of an initiative. It will be helpful to summarise the key elements of the cycle.

It is important to appreciate that the first three steps outlined above are best understood as setting the pre-conditions which allow the cycle of steps to be conducted in an informed manner. In other words, without a proper understanding of the values and components of community development, and an appreciation of the ABCD model on which the cycle described is based, effective practice will not be possible. Assuming that this understanding is in place, the cycle starts with the identification of the key stakeholders who are then engaged in definition of a shared vision, or sense of direction, related to the needs experienced. This vision should be understood, debated and shared between all the participants. It leads on to setting out the expected outcomes of a community development initiative. With such an understanding of vision and outcomes, we can turn to relating this clearly to the values and purposes of community development. Hence the vision is translated into clear statements relating the dimensions and elements of community empowerment to the improvement of the quality of community life (see section B). The specific inputs that will be made, processes that will be adopted and particular outputs which will be delivered are then identified. It is then necessary to identify the way in which information will be collected to measure progress and change. Finally, attention is given to identifying the lessons to be learned and feeding these into the continuing process of development.

Defining key terms

Since these terms are used extensively in this section it is important to be clear what is meant by input, process, output and outcome. The terms are discussed more fully in section C3.

- *Inputs* include the material resources of grants, premises and equipment. They also cover human resources – people's energy, motivation, time and commitment. Perhaps less obviously, the policies of government and other agencies, which locate and define the work, are equally significant. All these inputs may be found within communities and in the organisations working in or with them.

- *Processes* in community development are the ways in which the inputs are used to lead towards outcomes. They may include developing individual and organisational capacity, providing advice and support, encouraging reflection and planning, assessing power relationships and helping develop strategic thinking. In the ABCD model these processes are summarised as community empowerment.

- *Outputs* are the specific products of the processes, such as community organisations having access to information on funding sources, support to develop greater media skills, resources for childcare such as a local crèche. These outputs are matters that agencies have the capacity to deliver, hence their achievement is within their control. However, outputs are not ends in themselves but are the means to achieving changes that realise the vision of a better quality of community life. We call these the outcomes.

- *Outcomes* are the effects that we hope the processes and specific outputs will produce, for example, increased grant aid to community organisations, more influential community organisations, a safer community. Outcomes are not in the direct control of the community development agency or the community organisation because they are dependent on the actions of others. But their achievement is the means of delivering the vision of change that the community has defined.

The cycle of input–process–output–outcome can operate on short and long-term timescales. The outcome of one stage becomes an input to the new situation, and so the cycle repeats itself. An understanding of these ideas and relationships is fundamental to understanding how community development works.

Values in community development

The theory and practice of community development has always been informed by a set of values and principles. This value base is important in defining for whom and where its efforts are concentrated, the way it works with people, and the sorts of outcomes it seeks. The values of community development can be considered under three broad headings: what it challenges, the ideas it promotes, and the thinking it influences.

Community development challenges exclusion

Community development is committed to combating social exclusion, poverty, disadvantage and discrimination. As such, it should not be considered as a value-free or universal approach. It is based on a recognition that some people, some groups and some communities are excluded from social, economic and political opportunities for reasons of lack of wealth, cultural oppression, physical obstacles or prejudicial attitudes. The focus of community development is with groups and communities that are excluded due to one or more of these causes, and its role is to work with such groups to achieve change.

Thus community development promotes social inclusion. In emphasising the need to tackle the consequences of poverty, disadvantage and discrimination and to promote involvement and participation, social inclusion expresses ideas that have long been central to community development. Social inclusion can be promoted through the community development activities of providing support to the development of individual capacity, and building community capacity to generate social, economic and democratic activity and opportunities.

Achieving social inclusion is therefore an active process of people participation. It is not something that can be done to people but must be done with and by them. It is a participative and dynamic process of learning, action and reflection.

Community development promotes strong communities

The second set of values informs the way such change is understood. Community development reflects and promotes a number of ideas. These include:

Full citizenship

Many groups are effectively disenfranchised through the lack of opportunity to participate in decision making, or the failure of decision makers to recognise or respond to excluded voices. The idea of full or active citizenship recognises that the health of communities, and society as a whole, is enhanced when people are motivated and able to participate in meeting their needs. Active citizenship is not based on the idea of do-gooding or benevolent philanthropy but on ideas of mutuality and reciprocity which are the 'glue' that binds people together and underpins the very idea of society. The expression of shared responsibility evidenced in practical action is to be found in all dimensions of community life – politics, sport and recreation, care, art and culture, religion, the environment, health, economic development – and, at its best, involves participation across boundaries of race, age, gender and disability.

Community-led collective action

Community development is an approach to change that depends on building solidarity and support through emphasising the common aspects of individual problems and the capacity of people to work together in their common interest. The worker supports the development of community leadership and encourages the building of a collective, accountable approach. Collective action in communities includes small-scale and large-scale activities to meet local needs, as well as action to lobby for change.

Participative democracy

Widespread, active participation in public affairs is good in itself, as well as a means to achieving best value and effectiveness in administration of public services. A participative approach can lead to a better understanding of needs and issues, clarity about who benefits from, and who is excluded from, services, and can develop better ways of targeting scarce resources. It can also lead to innovative ways of meeting needs, including partnership arrangements through which communities can develop, administer and benefit from running services.

Empowerment

Most forms of exclusion are based on lack of power and influence, and imposed solutions are at best paternalistic and at worst oppressive. Community development has at its heart a commitment to empowerment: encouraging communities and groups to learn how power relationships operate, and to develop their ability to deal with the problems.

Problem focused learning

This is the core approach taken to empowerment. Community development is based on the idea that people learn from the experience of tackling their own problems. It seeks to encourage people to think about the causes of problems, act on those causes, and learn from the outcome. Similarly, policy on lifelong learning recognises that developing skill and understanding needs to be a continuing process. In part this reflects the value of continuous individual and community self-development and improvement. Equally it recognises that technological, social, economic, environmental and other forms of change require new skills and understanding. Hence lifelong learning is functional to the employability of individuals and the needs of the labour market and the national economy. It is also a source of personal fulfilment, achievement and self-realisation, and as such, a basis for building strong communities.

Preventative action

Much public service provision is based on dealing with problems after they have occurred. While recognising the importance of this, community development seeks to identify the underlying causes of problems and to deal with these, rather than with their manifestations. Strong communities have the capacity to identify potential problems and take preventative action.

Collaboration

Community development involves collaboration between interest groups, government and citizens. Some approaches to work in communities only emphasise self-help: what communities can do themselves in their own interest. Others seek to confront and challenge power holders directly. Neither approach leads to partnership or collaboration. Community development emphasises collaboration. Communities may be forced to adopt a confrontational position to get an issue recognised. Once the issues have been recognised, it is usually in the interests of both the community and the decision maker to identify and implement solutions. Similarly, many activities that start out as self-help will begin to engage with public agencies for funding or other forms of support. Once this happens some form of collaboration is almost inevitable. It is important to understand the strengths and weaknesses of communities (and other collaborators) in such relationships.

Community development influences policy

Finally, community development seeks to identify and define issues of public concern and inform and influence public policy in relation to those issues – which is a value in itself. It has a particular role in making the connections between private troubles and public issues. In doing so it reflects all the values discussed above, but seeks to reflect them in the way that public issues are identified, and in the way the formulation of policy is influenced.

Inputs, processes, outputs & outcomes

Inputs

Inputs mean the whole range of resources that are at the disposal of a community development programme. They are the tools and the ingredients that allow community development to take place. In ABCD we distinguish between inputs that are part of any community, and those that are brought in by outside bodies.

It is very important that communities and agencies recognise the wide range of inputs that contribute to the process of community development. Some will already be available within the community; more will be brought in by agencies working to support community development. Others may not be available immediately, but could be brought in with a little effort.

In community development it is essential to recognise that inputs are not simply the amount of budget controlled and applied by the main programme funder. To take this view undermines and marginalises the contribution that communities and other partners can make. Indeed, in terms of effort it is usually the community that makes the greatest investment and this is normally on an entirely voluntary basis. To focus on funds alone ignores the broader processes of community development and fails to recognise the contribution of a whole host of actors to the wider outcomes.

Inputs may not be available in a form that supports the process of community development. For example, community inputs of time may be compromised by internal conflict, and agency attention may be diverted by a sudden crisis elsewhere. Managing and maximising the value of inputs is thus a critical role in community development. It is for this reason that the recent review of community education in Scotland came to the conclusion that 'identifying and securing investment in community learning' – in other words, managing inputs – 'is one of the key roles of community education'.

Inputs from within communities

As we have noted, communities contribute enormously to community development: indeed without them the idea of community development would be a contradiction. But communities are not simply 'users' to be 'involved' in programmes. They have a whole range of inputs and resources that can be built into development programmes, whether in regeneration, health or housing. Ideally communities should be in the lead, defining what should happen and how. To reach this position should be an overriding aim of all community development programmes. At whatever stage, communities add value because of the resources they bring in. This contribution is sometimes called 'social capital' – the ability, energy, organisational capacity and commitment which people invest in community effort. While this jargon may be off-putting to some, it does at least confirm that community resources and relationships are crucial. Some of the main inputs that originate in communities are identified and considered in the following table.

Community inputs

Input	Issues
People	All communities are made up of people. Who are they, what are their concerns, what factors unify or divide them?
Time, motivation and energy	People in communities will devote an enormous amount of these invaluable assets to working for community change: provided that the change is in areas they feel passionate about, in work they believe will have real results, and where they believe their efforts will be recognised and valued in the community.
Skills, knowledge and understanding	Because they live there, people in communities bring extensive, unparalleled knowledge of community problems, resources and relationships, without which no community development programme would succeed. From experience they will often know what is likely to work and what is not. They will also know how best to engage with groups. These inputs are crucial.
Trust	Building a high level of trust within communities and between communities and other agents is crucial, and is a building block without which no change programme will succeed.
Community assets	The nature and role of community groups and organisations determines their input. Those that own assets in the community will be substantial stakeholders. In some cases their input will be quite extensive. It has been estimated, for example that the social economy – community organisations, local projects and other non-profit activities – is now the major employer in many former industrial areas.
Networks	As well as tangible assets, communities are in one sense a sum of interpersonal and intergroup relationships. In a well-functioning community these will be well-established and functional, and a crucial part of how the community actually works.
Leadership	There is sometimes a condescending view that communities lack leadership, and 'capacity-building' programmes are set in train to address this. Sometimes this analysis and action is appropriate, but at other times it is an unthinking response. The idea of leadership sometimes sits uneasily with community development ideas of inclusion and broad participation. But leadership is needed to realise these ideas, and is needed if communities are to engage fully in change.

Inputs from other stakeholders

A crucial part of the community development task is to identify the range of inputs that are already available, and others that might be accessed to maximise the value and effectiveness of the work. Stakeholders working with the community can bring in a wide range of inputs, and can also help access other resources and inputs from the external environment.

Other stakeholders' inputs

Input	Issues
A policy and strategic framework	Agencies normally engage with communities as part of some policy or strategy. These may be community development policies, or policies on health, housing, social care or other matters, that have an impact on the community. Partnerships are similar, although partners may have differing interests and priorities. For community development the crucial question is how far the relevant policies reflect community development principles, and how their implementation is managed. Policies and strategies can be audited from the perspective of whether they are likely to contribute to community empowerment.
Material resources	Funding for new facilities or to improve the quality of service is important. But there are always questions about where money comes from, what conditions are attached, what changes the money is expected to make, and who controls its allocation.
Co-ordination and partnership	A partnership approach is now virtually standard in community development. But how does a partnership view community activities that choose not to engage directly? How do partnerships view community development and community participation? Whose agenda leads, and how are the varied resources available to a partnership brought to bear?
Knowledge, support, training	Agencies can offer extensive contributions to community development: information, advice, access to technology and equipment, access to training and support.
People	As with communities, many agencies have individuals whose work requires or permits them to contribute time, energy and commitment to the community development process. They can offer contacts, information, encouragement, criticism and advice.

External inputs

Some stakeholders will be more directly involved in particular projects and programmes than others. It is important not to assume that this defines the significance of their inputs. Policy makers distanced from local concerns may, for example, have a major impact at local level without any awareness of the specific implications of their policies. Indeed some inputs may arise from sources that have no direct connection with local events and cannot be regarded as stakeholders. For example, general changes on the law on charitable status or child care practice may have significant local impact. Though some inputs are uncontrollable and unpredictable, understanding their impact is essential for planning and evaluation.

Processes

Processes are defined as those actions that need to take place to direct inputs towards desired outputs and outcomes. ABCD defines the central process of community development as community empowerment. It breaks this into the related processes of personal development, positive action, community organisation and using power. Workers and agencies whose role includes assisting community empowerment are centrally concerned with building the capacity of communities and the skills, knowledge and confidence of individuals in the community. These activities can be planned, evaluated and improved, and the Scottish Community Development Council has produced a framework for this – Learning Evaluation and Planning (LEAP) – which draws on the thinking behind ABCD.[7]

Outputs

As we have seen, outputs are the direct products of a community development process. They are the actions that can be planned using the available inputs, for example, organising a community conference, providing an information service, carrying out a community survey, running a training course, setting up an after-school care club. As such, they are within the control of the individual, agency or group that provides and supports them. They are set because they are believed to have the potential to lead to wider change. They can be quantified (for example, the number of places available in an after-school facility), or measured qualitatively (for example, the provision of a secure environment for children in an after-school facility).

One of the major flaws in community development has been a tendency to plan and evaluate in terms of outputs as if they were ends in themselves. Knowing what the outputs are intended to be, ensuring that the inputs are there to enable their delivery, and knowing whether the outputs have been delivered are all essential. But this is not sufficient. We need to know what difference they make and what impact they have on the problems we set out to tackle.

Outcomes

Outcomes are the effects of outputs such as those described above. For example, the community survey provides information that may enable local people to define problems more clearly and argue for better solutions, the information service may empower people to seek their rights and improve their quality of life. Such outcomes are sought by, but not in the direct control of the individual, agency or group that seeks to bring them about. They are subject to choices, decisions and influences of people and institutions over which the immediate stakeholders do not have control.

As with outputs, outcomes may be both quantifiable (for example, more parents taking up job opportunities as a result of the after-school facility providing places), or essentially qualitative (for example, the heightened self-esteem that children attending the centre may develop).

The crucial point in relation to community development is that the outcomes it seeks are almost always wider than the outputs it can control and influence. So, an after-school facility may seek to enhance the self-esteem of the children who attend, but whether self-esteem is in fact developed is the product of a wider range of individual, family and social factors than simply attendance at the facility. However, given that community development is largely concerned with wider outcomes that it cannot control, the relationship between the outputs that it can influence and the wider outcomes is crucial to understand. Planning, evaluation and learning depend on our ability to have good information, and to be able to make judgements about how far community development activities have indeed led to the wider outcomes that are sought.

The ABCD model

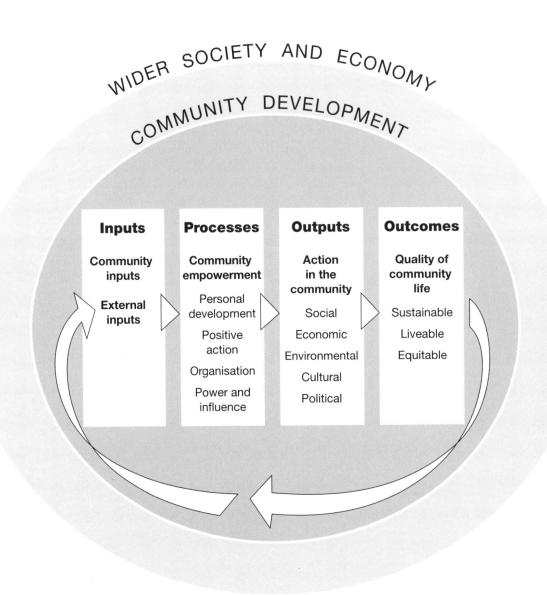

WIDER SOCIETY AND ECONOMY

COMMUNITY DEVELOPMENT

Inputs	Processes	Outputs	Outcomes
Community inputs	Community empowerment	Action in the community	Quality of community life
External inputs	Personal development	Social	Sustainable
	Positive action	Economic	Liveable
	Organisation	Environmental	Equitable
	Power and influence	Cultural	
		Political	

Understanding the model

The model above illustrates that community development operates within a wider social, economic and political context. It locates the inputs from both within and outside the community, as discussed in C3. It shows how community empowerment is the core process of community development, and that this leads to outputs relating to changes in social, environmental, economic, cultural or political issues. These in turn lead to outcomes in the quality of community life. The aim is that communities should be sustainable, liveable and equitable. Changes in the quality of life affect the nature of the community and external inputs, making the whole process cyclical, as represented by the arrows.

A number of further points can be made. First, it is important to remind ourselves that community development can relate to communities of place, such as neighbourhoods, housing estates or villages, to communities of identity, in which people share a common culture or set of beliefs, or to communities bound by common interests, for example users of a particular service.

It can be seen that community development operates within the context of wider society, and thus must recognise and respond to its social, economic, technological, cultural and policy influence. For example, an economic downturn, a change in government or a shift in cultural values about the family would each have an impact on community development work. Clearly, community development also operates within a local context. For example, a series of overlapping regeneration or health programmes in an area will have an impact on community development, as will the expression of racism in a locality.

Looking at the inputs to community development, we can see that these include inputs from the community itself – such as people's energy and motivation, their networks and relationships and their own assets, as well as inputs from outside the community. These might include grants, access to resources, or policies and strategies with impact on the community. Both types of input have been discussed in C3. It is important to note that inputs can have positive or negative effects.

Turning to process, the model shows that community development has the process objective of community empowerment. The empowerment process can be described as the way in which inputs are used to develop the ability of the community to achieve change. While this is essentially a process, it is important to realise that an empowered community is also an outcome. Community empowerment has four components, or dimensions – personal empowerment, positive action, community organisation and participation and involvement. Each is described in detail in sections B1 to B4.

Community development has planned outputs that can be achieved and evaluated directly. The outputs will be specific actions that relate to economic, social, environmental, cultural or political issues in communities. Community development activity relates to all these spheres, and these are described in more detail in sections B6 to B10. The outputs are chosen and designed with the intention of achieving particular outcomes that reflect the overall vision of change that the stakeholders have identified.

The outcomes are the wider consequences of the outputs although there are wider influences on their achievement. They relate to improvement in the quality of community life. The quality of life in communities reflects the cultural, social, political, environmental and economic factors in relation to which outputs have been addressed. Improvements in the quality of community life potentially have an impact on the wider economy and society. The outcomes that community development seeks should be consistent with its underpinning values. Hence it sets out to establish more equitable, sustainable and liveable communities. This is discussed further in B11.

Community development is a progressive activity – each change leads to new understandings, relationships and actions – the model must therefore be seen as dynamic, hence the circular direction of the arrows.

Equipped with a basic understanding of community development as a cycle of change, with inputs, processes, outputs and outcomes as the basic concepts, we can begin to use the model to address some of the crucial questions in planning and evaluating community development. These questions include:

- what are the inputs to community development activity, and how do they change with the progress of action?

- how well are the inputs applied to the process of community empowerment?

- how is the empowerment process used to influence the quality of community life?

- what influence does an empowered community have on the quality of community life, i.e. what are the outputs and outcomes?

- how do the changes and lessons learned affect the empowerment process and the inputs to it?

Overall, the model emphasises continuous change over time both in the way in which change occurs and the nature of that change.

Stakeholders

Planning and evaluating community development cannot take place in isolation. All those involved – or potentially involved – should participate because they have an interest (or stake) in what happens. Such a stake may be because of their involvement as a contributor, or because they stand to gain or lose from the activity. Such participation is a basic value of community development. Thus, every community development programme has stakeholders: people, groups and agencies who have a material interest in the process and outcome of the programme, and some influence over its shape and direction. It is important that programmes recognise the range of stakeholders involved, and assess their capacity to influence the outcome.

Stakeholders are defined as all those people who have an *active* interest in the inputs, process, outputs and outcomes of community development activity. Such stakeholders will include:

- community members
- community groups and organisations, including committee members and staff
- workers and managers in voluntary and statutory agencies working with the community
- resource provides and funders
- policy makers and programme managers.

Involving the stakeholders cannot be a token gesture. If communities and agencies are to work together in real partnership both need to develop and share a sense of engagement, commitment and trust. To achieve this may not be easy, but the attempt must be made. Each of the stakeholders will need to recognise the others' role and authority, and accommodate their different perspectives. Negotiation will often be needed over priorities, commitment of resources, timescales, methods of working and expected outcomes. In most cases, stakeholders are motivated to participate because they recognise that joint working is likely to be more effective in achieving their aims. To bring this added value, they need to recognise that there must be a trade-off, involving them in using resources to support the achievement of outcomes desired by other partners.

In all this it is important to remember the 'first among equals' status of community participants, reflecting the values of community development. There may be substantial inequities affecting the ability of some stakeholders – especially community representatives – to participate. They are often the least well resourced, but are often required to make the greatest personal investment. Whereas agency staff are paid to be involved, and elected members have their expenses covered, community representatives often have to give large amounts of time on an entirely voluntary basis. Community representatives do not normally have access to the administrative, information and research services that agencies have, and are often less familiar than the agencies with procedures of meetings. Other barriers are language, access, childcare, being undervalued and being excluded from the places where the 'real' decisions are made. Community development initiatives need to be aware of all these factors, and invest in providing the support needed for effective community participation. This should help equalise the relationship between stakeholders.

In thinking about stakeholders, it is important to consider the resources – or inputs – they may be able to contribute to the process of change. Bear in mind that inputs can be tangible (funds, policies, equipment, premises, information), or intangible (energy, enthusiasm, commitment, volunteers' time). We have already looked at this in some detail in section C3. There we discussed how inputs can originate from both within and outside the community. Some may be positive contributions to the process of change, while others may be obstacles. The task of community development is to maximise the potential value of all the inputs to the process of change. To do this successfully involves several challenges:

- negotiating between stakeholders' different expectations and requirements
- maintaining relationships that enable services to be delivered successfully, while supporting the community development process
- acknowledging and dealing with conflicts of interest, political sensitivities and representation.

Whatever stakeholder interest you come from, you will need to ask some basic questions:

— Who are the potential stakeholders – projects, volunteers/community activists, committee members, agency staff, agency managers, service users, politicians, funders?

— Why should they be involved?

— What might they contribute, and what are the benefits to them?

— Which stakeholders might have a negative influence, and how could this be counteracted?

Clearly, the stakeholders involved will be specific to each community development activity, and their role in relation to the activity will vary. But for effective practice their collaboration needs to be nurtured.

Briefing the stakeholders in community development

As discussed in section A3, the stakeholders do not always have or share a view about what community development is, or why it is important. It is useful to be able to provide the arguments in favour of adopting the approach. Many of the key points have been made in section A of the handbook. This shows how an understanding of the links between planning, evaluation and learning, and a critical approach to work can be informed by using ABCD. For community and voluntary groups the model provides a framework within which work can be planned, and a way to check how and whether progress is made. The emphasis on involving stakeholders also encourages critical questions to be raised about who is involved and on what terms. Adopting such an approach is likely to ensure the most effective use of scarce resources, and to hold the various partners and stakeholders accountable to each other.

Similar arguments can be advanced at programme and policy level, in particular by emphasising the links between community development and the need for professional agencies to engage more closely with the communities with whom they work.

Vision

In this section we discuss the importance of establishing a long-term vision that the stakeholders share and explore how this is related to outcomes.

What do we mean by vision? We are talking about development of a long-term view of the overall changes necessary to meet the aspirations of the stakeholders. The vision will present a clear and better alternative to present circumstances, that will improve the quality of personal and community life. The vision should represent the sum total of the outcomes sought.

Some people in community development reject the idea of 'vision' or 'mission' as being too directive, too tied into management thinking or too task focused. Others hold that it is pointless to define a desired future state because we can neither predict nor determine what will happen. At the same time, there are too many community development initiatives that express their aims in vague or unrealistic ways, leaving both workers and community members unclear about what they are trying to do.

ABCD suggests a middle course. It recognises that the stakeholders enter into a community development initiative with a wide range of – sometimes conflicting – purposes. The initiative will fail if the stakeholders do not make their expectations explicit, resolve their conflicting interests and agree with each other where the initiative should lead. Working to establish a vision helps identify and explore differences between partners, and encourages each to reconsider its position in light of the perspective of others.

It should be acknowledged that there will be times when stakeholders fail to reach an agreed vision. There may, for example, be irreconcilable conflict within the community, or major differences between a community's view of its involvement and the view of a local authority. Even here, the attempt to establish a vision will have exposed these differences, and perhaps encouraged either a new agenda or the establishment of a new coalition of stakeholders.

More positively, developing a 'vision' between the stakeholders can also encourage a more creative and dynamic approach. The sum of the partnership which emerges should be greater than the individual parts. Bringing together different resources and skills which complement one another can stimulate new ways of thinking about what may be possible in communities and how it may be done.

However, visioning change will only be a helpful activity if it is tempered by realism on the part of all stakeholders. A vision that does not relate to the inputs which can actually be made or requires adoption of processes of action or specific outputs which the stakeholder lacks the knowledge or skills to deliver, will lead to frustration and failure (see section C8). The proofing of the vision against the capacity, opportunity and motivation of the stakeholders to deliver it is an essential activity. This is not to suggest that we should be content with a limited vision, but to assert the importance of ensuring that if we have identified gaps in our capacity then we have planned for how these can be filled.

Various techniques are available to help communities and agencies work together to build a vision for the future (see the Tools for Change manual[8] and the ABCD Resource Pack[9]). The key issue is to ensure that all the stakeholders are involved, and that the vision is underpinned by an understanding of the resources that each stakeholder can bring to the initiative.

Using the ABCD model, section B of the handbook can be used to check the relationship between a vision and the dimensions of community development. It can, for example, prompt a consideration of whether all the dimensions of community empowerment are included, or whether the links between the different components of the quality of community life have been recognised. Having referred to section B, it should be possible to express the vision of an initiative in terms of community development outcomes.

Dimensions, elements and indicators

Having identified the vision and the intended outcomes at the general level, for practical purposes of planning, implementation and evaluation it is essential to move to more detailed specification of what will be involved. The material in section B is designed to assist you to do this. It sets out the key *dimensions* of community development – four for community empowerment, and five for the quality of community life. Each dimension is then broken down into *elements*. An element is essentially a statement that is sufficiently specific that it can be measured, whether directly or indirectly. Elements may be measured quantitatively or qualitatively.

Section B goes on to suggest some 'measures of change' that can be used to gain an understanding of what is happening in an initiative. These can be direct *measures* or indirect *indicators* of change:

— A *measure* is a quantified description of outputs or performance. Measures apply where there is a clear and direct relationship between the way in which the inputs are applied, the outputs they produce and outcomes that result. Cause and effect can be clearly traced.

— An *indicator* is a proxy measure used when output or performance is not directly measurable. Indicators apply where cause and effect cannot be so clearly traced. Indicators suggest, but do not prove a causal relationship – there may be many other influences involved. Evidence that a causal relationship exists is reinforced when several indicators suggest the same explanation. They relate closely to the elements, and enable assessment of whether and how change is occurring in relation to a given element.

We need measures and indicators to identify the information that will help us understand:

● what has changed

● why or how it has changed

● who has benefited

● how else it might have been done

● how closely change reflects plans

● how the inputs were used.

In community development we are often able to use measures in relation to outputs, but outcomes are more frequently assessed with the use of indicators.

It is important to note that measures are not always quantitative, nor are indicators always qualitative. Since the outputs of community development are mainly a way to achieve wider outcomes, gaining evidence in relation to outcomes is essential to effective evaluation. To do so, we are likely to be more dependent on indicators than measures because there is likely to be a wide range of influences that may affect the evidence we can gather.

In choosing the measures and indicators for a programme, it is important to think about:

— Whether to look at a few items in detail or seek a broader view.

— How easy it will be to collect information on each measure. Easily available information is not necessarily the most useful. For example, counting heads at a meeting is easy but says nothing about the outcome or value of the meeting. Finding this out is harder, but more valuable.

— How to get information about the wider effects of a programme. A broader range of measures and indicators will pick up such broader perspectives.

— How to achieve a balance between quantity (how much is done), quality (how well it is done) and equity (fairness, or who benefits). You should aim to get all three sorts of information.

Once you have worked through the steps described you should have an understanding of the stakeholders in your initiative, the vision of how you intend things to change, a statement of this in terms of the outputs you can achieve and the wider outcomes you intend them to lead to. All this will be summarised in a chosen list of elements that relate to the dimensions of community empowerment and the quality of community life.

Once the dimensions and elements of community development on which your work will focus are clear, it is essential to give attention to precisely how it will be delivered. This requires agreement about different stakeholders' inputs, processes or methods of working to be adopted and specific outputs to be delivered. All of this is designed to achieve the intended outcomes.

This step concerns how agencies and community groups will be engaged in the achievement of change, the level of investment that will be made and by whom. Though ultimately community learning must be measured by its outcomes it is essential to know what the relationship is between the methods used, the investment made and the outcomes which result. Your evaluation therefore needs to encompass assessment of the inputs, processes and outputs.

Decisions about inputs, processes and output are interactive. Action must respond to needs but also be realistic about available inputs. Hence, there is a need to find a balance between inputs, processes and output. Whilst outputs and processes should be realistic they also have to be worthwhile and relevant to the achievement of the intended outcomes.

Inputs should be quantified and monitored for quality; the outputs of the processes adopted should be measurable and time scaled.

Getting information

Information is needed for two purposes:

- to identify conditions in relation to the agreed indicators at the start of an initiative, or at a particular point within it: we call the starting point the baseline
- to provide evidence of change.

Data is therefore needed at the start of evaluation and should be collected continuously in the process of the work. In community development it is important to ensure that the way information is collected is consistent with its values. It should thus be participative, empowering and readily understandable. For evaluation to be an effective tool for development, it must be efficient and not interfere with the process of the work. There are three basic ways to get information:

- to observe
- to ask questions
- to consult existing records.

No one approach will meet all needs, so it is normal to choose more than one method. The advantages and disadvantages of each approach, and some of the ways they could be used, are discussed below.

Observation

In this approach, the evaluator is present, watches events and actions, and writes down, films or tape-records what happens. Actually being there has obvious benefits. There are some problems, though. First, by being present, the observer may affect what happens. Second, it can be hard to observe and take accurate notes at the same time. Third, what the observer records may be biased by his or her own views of what is important.

Other sources of information are based on observation. For example, the records of meetings taken by participants will be based on their own observations.

Observation can be undertaken in a participant or non-participant fashion. It allows you to collect evidence directly, but requires you to be present when the key events occur. Observation can be a useful way to build hypotheses which can be subsequently tested using other types of information.

Asking questions

Asking questions is a good way of finding out information and getting a range of comments from people involved in or affected by a programme. There are many ways it can be done:

— Written questionnaires, ranging from formal ones with tick boxes, to informal ones which invite general comments and responses. They can be used with funders, workers or community members.

— Asking individuals questions face to face. Again, the approach may be formal or informal, and it could be used with any of the interested parties.

— A very powerful form of questioning, which is often used in community development evaluation, is to work with groups. These may be existing community organisations, members of several organisations, or mixed groups of community members, project workers and programme managers. The advantage is that this allows different views to be expressed, discussed and explored. It can be a good way of getting a sophisticated view of what is happening. There are many methods available to maximise involvement in such group evaluation, and to make sure every voice is heard.

Surveys can be used as a good way to collect facts and opinions from a wide range of people. They can provide powerful quantified results, and can be structured to ensure that the views of minorities are sought and represented. They can be reasonably straightforward to plan and analyse, and they can help an organisation take ownership of a local issue by being seen to be doing something about it. But they are of less value in getting into more detailed opinion and insight, and can be expensive if they aim to get a wide cross-section of views rather than a sample.

Group discussions and consultations are valuable if you need a collective answer, or want to see how people react to suggestions. They are also useful for developing ideas and gaining a detailed insight into an issue. However, they cannot produce such a wide cross-section of views as other methods and will not produce readily quantifiable information. They also require considerable skills to organise, run and record.

Whatever method you use, it is good practice to:

— Use a wide range of methods: focus groups, consultations, interviews and feedback sessions.

— Be welcoming and use diversity: get a mix of views and perspectives.

— Be focused: ask relevant questions about a specific activities.

— Keep it as simple as possible.

— Look for emerging themes: interpret findings and plan suitable actions and interventions.

— Offer choices and options: asking people to rank the importance of items can be more effective than asking 'what is important?'

— Remember that views change: as people develop confidence and new skills their expectations shift.

— Use innovative techniques: videos and tapes, photographs, exhibitions, drama and arts, physical representation, graffiti walls, diagrams, story telling, group techniques (see 'Tools for Change').

Consulting existing records

A lot of useful information will already be available, although it is not always easy to get. Census information, agency statistics, funding applications, policy documents, records of meetings and newspaper reports all have their place. However, they are not written for the purposes of evaluation so they will not always provide the right sort of information. If you intend to use existing records it is important to think about how they will be used and how readily they are available.

Projects and programmes can help themselves by setting up a good internal recording system. This can include project plans, reports on meetings and reviews, weekly or monthly records of activity and progress, reports to committees or funders, reports on resources, and information about the community with which it is working. Guidelines are available to help projects with this type of recording.

Planning information collection

Before embarking on the collection of information it is important to be clear about:

- what type of information you want: facts, figures, opinions or perceptions
- who you want the information from: users, individual residents, community representatives, workers, the community in general
- what resources you have: time, money, people
- what skills you need access to: questionnaire design, interviewing, group facilitation, data analysis.

Who will collect information and how

It is useful to think about what information may already exist and how it can be used, as well as what new information needs to be gathered. The task of gathering information is one that can often best be done by community members, and the managers of re-generation programmes should be encouraged to consider this possibility. For some people it can be a route to employment, but it is in any case an effective way to ensure that the performance of regeneration initiatives is well monitored, by people who will have the ear of community members.

The baseline: when and how to start

In order to measure any changes or progress, we need to know where we started from. What are the conditions at the beginning of the evaluation of the policy, programme or project and what will any changes be measured against? Baselines can only be set once we have identified the measures and indicators to be used. Thus, to establish baseline information, you should assess the conditions using the agreed indicators and the identified methods of collecting information. As well as giving you an understanding of where things are at and what you may need to do, collecting baseline information also provides an opportunity to test out the value and applicability of your indicators, and of the methods you plan to use.

Change can be measured while an activity is in progress. This is known as **formative evaluation**. This informs our understanding of what is happening, as it happens. Change can also be measured at the end of a process. This is called **summative evaluation**, and provides an overview of what has been achieved and the lessons learned.

With formative evaluation it may be helpful to choose regular time intervals to assess progress, or to identify significant stages in planning or carrying out the work. If regular formative evaluation takes place as part of an integrated work process, then the data required for a summative evaluation will be available without the need for significant extra resources.

Assessing change over time may show that what has happened is different from what was intended or anticipated. This may arise because of **goal displacement** – an often unconscious change of direction resulting from blocks and difficulties. Or it may be a result of **goal succession** – a deliberate redefinition of goals based on successful achievement of what was intended. Evaluation should take note of both possibilities.

Assessing evidence, drawing conclusions, learning lessons

In this section we explore issues that arise from applying the model to real world policies, programmes and projects. ABCD can help you to answer critical questions about your performance:

- are the intended outputs delivered?
- do these lead to the intended outcomes?
- what other outcomes result?
- from the perspective of all the stakeholders are these outcomes desirable?
- in the context of the values and principles of community learning are the outcomes desirable?
- were the outcomes achieved efficiently and effectively?
- what has been learned?
- how will lessons learned influence, in future, the inputs that are made, the outputs which are provided and the outcomes which are sought?

It can be helpful to think about the different types of insights that can be gained from a review of evidence. Consideration can focus on:

- inputs: asking whether all potential inputs became available and were used effectively
- process: whether and how empowerment took place, and how the various stakeholders contributed to change
- outputs: what was the quality and quantity
- outcomes: how did things change and what were the key factors
- learning: have new ideas or innovations been found and tested?

Evaluation should not be seen as an event. It is an activity that should inform the development and direction of community development as a process on a continuing basis. Hence it should be integral to all practice. Evaluation is not an additional chore: it is a core part of practice itself. Without it we lack reference points to make critical judgements about where we should be going, how we should be going about it and where we have got to.

Achieving
Better
Community
Development

d1 **A worked example**..*page 77*

A worked example

In this section we illustrate the application of the materials in the handbook through a hypothetical example – the WEANS project. (For the uninitiated, 'weans' is Scottish vernacular for children!)

WEANS – Weavers End After-School Neighbourhood Support – is an after-school care club. We will follow through its development and illustrate how the planning and evaluation of its work drew on the ABCD framework. In order to do this we will review the steps identified in section C1: Stages in community development.

WEANS developed from an initiative in Weavers End taken by an inter-faith community development group. Weavers End is an inner city area with a diverse ethnic population. Concerned about racism and poverty in the community an initiative was developed between faith groups including the Catholic church, two protestant churches, the mosque and the Sikh temple.

The catholic priest had attended a part-time post-qualifying training course in community development at a local university and believed that this approach could be beneficial for the neighbourhood. As part of the course he had been introduced to the ABCD framework and decided that this might be helpful in Weavers End. Initially he called together a meeting of leaders of the faith groups to explore with them the possible benefits of community development. In turn this group organised a community conference to enable members of each group to participate in a discussion of community needs and the potential of community development. In this way *step 1* was taken.

Whilst it was felt to be important to recognise the cultural and religious identities and customs of all the faith groups the community conference nonetheless felt that a joint initiative to promote community co-operation and development would be desirable. Given a recent history of inter-racial conflicts between young people, this was a common concern among participants. A decision was taken to set up a steering group for an initiative focusing on children and young people in the community. The primary task of this group was to take *step 2* by exploring what the key components of community development were and what this might mean in Weavers End. The group would report to a recall community conference two months later.

The working group was supported by the Catholic priest. He introduced the ideas associated with the ABCD model, hence *step 2* and *step 3* were combined. At its first meeting the group was invited to participate in an exercise in which they identified the things that they thought characterised a *healthy community* for children and young people. They considered what would make for a *liveable*, *equitable* and *sustainable* community (see section B11). By doing this they were beginning to think about the kinds of *outcomes* that a community initiative might have. Particularly important features included:

- opportunities for personal learning, development and recreation which would enhance equity

- improving relationships between ethnic groups to create a safer, more sustainable and equitable community

- reducing the risk of anti-social or criminal behaviour, including drug misuse, which would promote a more liveable and sustainable community.

After this meeting members were invited to reflect on what sorts of activities in the community might help to create the kind of community that they thought was desirable and who might be able to contribute to them. The following meeting reviewed the ideas of the members. Several options were suggested:

- a summer play-scheme

- a youth club

- a youth café

- an after-school care club.

These were potential *outputs* that might be sought because they might help to achieve the *outcomes* that had been identified previously.

The group then considered what *inputs* might be available. From the community they felt that potentially there would be people with skills, knowledge, motivation and leadership capacity for an initiative but that this would need to be tested out. They knew that the Catholic church was prepared to use its hall. The leaders of the inter-faith group had already committed themselves to pooling funding to pump-prime an initiative but it was clear that there would need to be additional funds. Possible sources included the local authority, the lottery charities board and local trust funds.

The group considered how an initiative should be developed. Thus they looked at *processes* and concluded that they would need to ensure that the development would need to adopt an empowering approach to children and young people as well as the adults involved. They realised that this could not happen unless the development was based on:

- participation and collaboration with other partners

- promotion of a community owned and run organisation

- positive action to ensure that all groups in the community could be involved.

In the light of these discussions the working group fed back its ideas to the recall community conference. The conference decided that an after-school care club for primary school age children was a priority, not only because there was a need to support children and families through such a service, but also because it was felt that working with younger children from different ethnic groups would build a base for more harmonious community relations in the long term. Participants not only felt that the community had the motivation but that there was more confidence, experience and skills to develop this project than the others suggested by the working group.

Volunteers interested in contributing to the club were invited to identify themselves. Over 30 people put their names forward. The name Weavers End After-School Neighbourhood Support (WEANS) was adopted. These volunteers agreed to meet again to discuss the idea with the working group members and form a formal steering group. Community work support would be provided by the Catholic priest. For these new participants to develop an effective project it would be important for them to explore what the ideas involved in community development are. Since they had found it helpful, the working group used the ABCD framework for planning and evaluation. In effect what was happening was that stages 1–3 were being repeated to ensure that new participants could think about what they wanted to achieve, what they would actually do and what would enable this to happen. The working group realised that, though the ABCD manual had talked about 9 steps, the real world was not quite as neat and tidy. For new participants, missing out the early steps would be problem. Once it was established, WEANS was to find that it often repeated or revisited steps with new partners and participants. However, on some occasions new partners were already familiar with community development ideas and did not need to have the ABCD model explained – for them steps 1–3 were not needed because they had been completed elsewhere.

To help the new volunteers to get involved the working group began by thinking about how to do this. The working group had initially found it quite difficult to think about inputs, outputs processes and outcomes. They realised that this can apply to many every-day situations and that an analogy might help new participants grasp the ideas more quickly. They used the analogy of making an apple pie.

To make an apple pie needs certain **inputs**: the motivation of the cook, the recipe, the ingredients, and the availability of an oven. The quality of each of these will have a significant impact on the quality of the final product. The **process** of making the pie in-cludes following the recipe, preparing the apples, mixing the pastry, setting the oven and baking the pie for the required time at the required temperature. Again the quality of these processes will affect the result. The **output** is the pie itself: and the nature of the output can be measured for consistency, size, taste. The **outcome** is the result of the pie. Did people eat it, did they enjoy it, did the dog steal it? Outcomes may be intended or unintended, but can be hard to control.

Thinking about apple pies helped them to understand the ideas behind planning and evaluation. Using the analogy they reviewed the ideas that the working group had pro-duced. They felt that they provided a broad direction for development but that they would now need to be clearer about what outcomes they were hoping to achieve and the way in which they would develop activities which could help them happen. However, they were also aware from the discussion of inputs and processes that as yet they did not have all the people involved who would need to make inputs. This led to a review of who the **stakeholders** would be. In doing this the group was focusing on the first part of *step 4*, identifying stakeholders.

They realised that, as yet, some stakeholders had not been involved at all and that assumptions might be being made about their views and interests. In particular they realised that the children themselves and their parents needed to be involved in thinking about what the after-school project might do. Similarly they realised that the project would be much more likely to succeed if it was developed in collaboration with the local primary school. They realised it was necessary to complete step 4 by working directly with the stakeholders and move on to *step 5* which would involve working on a shared vision for change within which specific outcomes would be identified. The newly formed steering group would take this on.

It was decided that contact needed to be made with other potential stakeholders and that, providing the school head-teacher was supportive, the obvious route was through the school.

Fortunately the head-teacher was interested in the idea because it might assist with improving children's school performance and help to tackle social exclusion (this was a priority of her education authority). A meeting was arranged. It was agreed that an event would be held in the school on a Saturday morning for children, parents, teachers, representatives of the faith groups and members of the steering group. The purpose would be to move on with the stakeholders to setting a vision and defining outcomes for WEANS.

To involve children and adult community members and agency workers in the same process is difficult. The steering group heard that another group had used the image of a tree to help people to think about what needed to be done. Inputs are the sun and rain, nutrients in the soil and the seed from which the tree grows. Processes, represented in the trunk of the tree, are those things that help the tree grow, including the way it is tended by a gardener. Outputs are leaves and fruit, while outcomes are those things made possible by the existence of the tree: you can sit in its shade, birds can nest in it, or children can play in it.

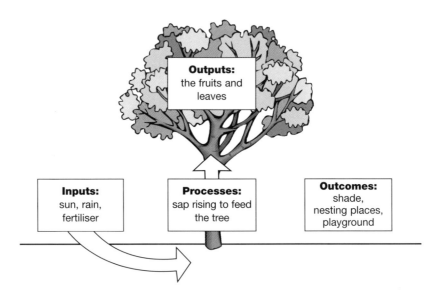

The steering group thought that creating the tree could be the focus of the event. Children and parents could be involved in an arts workshop which would create a large model tree. Once created, they asked all the participants to think of the tree as the WEANS project, and to write on adhesive slips of paper – first all the 'outcomes': things happening in the community that the project could contribute to. They then looked at the 'inputs': the things that the project needed in order to develop and keep going; then the 'processes': the ways that the centre could empower users and the community, and what the staff, volunteers and other supporters could do to make the project work; then the 'outputs': the actual activities and actions of the project. This exercise helped them see much more clearly how the project might be developed.

Having discussed all the questions that the exercise raised, the steering group produced the diagram opposite, that set out the way in which the inputs processes and outputs of WEANS could contribute to wider outcomes in the community.

Inputs	Processes	Outputs	Outcomes
Skills, knowledge, motivation of community volunteers	A community run project with a democratic constitution providing for election of a management committee and office bearers to organise a rota of volunteers to provide the service	An after school care service open to all children of primary school age, providing:	Reduced racism and more co-operation and respect between ethnic and religious groups
Support of faith group leaders including pump priming grant		— A secure environment for children	Reduced bullying
			Reduced young offending
Specific support from Catholic priest		— A homework club	
	Advice and information from Catholic priest, the school and faith group leaders	— A sports programme	Children achieving their potential and better school performance
Premises provided by Catholic church			
Support from head-teacher and school staff		— An arts and drama programme	Improved health of children
	Training for volunteers	— A healthy eating project	Parents more able to enter the job market and reduced poverty
	Networking with other after-school care projects		Reduced family stress
			Increased confidence and capacity of community

By doing this exercise, the group identified both what it was hoping to achieve and how it would go about it. It had highlighted inputs, processes and outputs leading to outcomes relating to the quality of community life ant the empowerment of community members. At this point they moved to *step 6*. This step would enable them to review their plan employing the dimensions of community development set out in the ABCD framework and move on to identify indicators which would help them to evaluate whether they were making progress in relation to outcomes and securing the inputs and processes to deliver their intended outputs.

To do this WEANS steering group considered the products of the stakeholder visioning exercise. They looked at each of the nine dimensions of community development identified in section B of this handbook, and plotted their processes, outputs and outcomes accordingly.

ABCD dimension	WEANS processes and outputs	WEANS possible outcome
Empowerment:		
Personal empowerment	Advice, information and training to committee and volunteers	Children achieving their potential
Positive action	Homework club	Better school performance
Community organisation	Democratically constituted WEANS; networking with other after school projects	Increased confidence and capacity of community
Participation and involvement	Volunteers and community leaders running WEANS	Increased co-operation between ethnic and religious groups
Quality of Life:		
Community economic development		Potential for parents to enter labour market and potential impact on family income
Social and service development		Reduced family stress
Community health and safety	Sports programme; healthy eating programme; secure environment for children	Reduced young offending Improved health
Community arts and culture	Arts and drama programme	Children achieving their potential
Governance and development		

Having done this classification the group were able to make some observations. First they had had some difficulty in deciding which box to put the outputs and outcomes in. For example, the homework club could have been seen as a personal development output, but the group decided to classify it as a positive action output as they saw it primarily as a way of supporting children who sometimes felt excluded from mainstream school activity. There is thus no 'right' box – but the process of choosing can offer new insights into what is being planned.

Second, they looked at the gaps in the boxes. In the four community empowerment dimensions they were pleased to note that they had met all four, given that ABCD insists that all of these dimensions are a necessary part of community development. However, there were no entries under governance and development. They reminded themselves that projects may only address some of the quality of life dimensions.

Third, they noted that there was not necessarily a direct relationship between a particular output and the overall outcomes. For example, under the economic development dimension they noted that the centre could have a positive impact on the possibility that parents could get work, and thus have a potential effect on family income. Yet they listed no specific outputs under the economic development dimension. Similarly, though it was hoped that there would be social benefits from reduced family stress no one output was linked to this specifically. From this they realised that there could be both direct and indirect outcomes of their work. This is a common feature of community development initiatives.

The next task was to use the ABCD framework to think about measures and indicators that they might use to evaluate the progress that they were making.

Reviewing what was planned, the WEANS stakeholders realised that it would be impractical to monitor and evaluate every possible aspect of their work. They needed to decide which areas were the most important to them, and to focus the evaluation on these areas. They were aware that they would need systems in place to record and monitor their activities: the number of children attending, the involvement of parents at open meetings, the patterns of children's interest in the homework support, sports, arts and healthy eating projects. They decided that they would concentrate on the areas of their work that they thought might have the most significant impact on the community as a whole and thus agreed that they would look at two areas in detail:

- The relationship between the safe and secure environment they were seeking to maintain, and disturbances involving children (such as vandalism, shoplifting, bullying, inter-ethnic fighting) in the neighbourhood.

- The quality of the relationship between ethnic groups in the community.

Having identified these two key areas they turned their attention to how they would know whether and how things were changing. They realised that it was usually possible to find direct measures of whether an output had been delivered because there was a direct and traceable relationship between inputs made, processes adopted and what actually happened. However, it was often more difficult to be certain what the cause of outcome changes actually was. Other things than the WEANS project could often be equally important. Here they would have to rely more heavily on indicators. If several indicators suggested a connection with the activities of WEANS this could be taken as evidence that it was being effective but single indicators would not be enough. They found identifying measures and indicators easier in relation to area 1 than area 2 because the outcome itself was more tangible and quantifiable.

They came up with two sets of measures and indicators, shown overleaf.

Area 1:

Measures and indicators of outputs	Measures and indicators of outcomes
Quantitative:	**Quantitative:**
1 Number of children regularly attending WEANS relative to the potential number	7 Number of complaints about vandalism, fighting and shoplifting received by local police
2 Amount of time which children spend in different recreation or learning activities in WEANS	8 Improved educational performance of children in school
3 Independent audit information on health and safety	9 Number of complaints received by school about bullying
Qualitative:	**Qualitative:**
4 Satisfaction expressed by children about the quality of the service	10 Observed self confidence, behaviour and motivation of the children in the community
5 Satisfaction expressed by parents about the quality of the service	11 Comments of parents about children's self confidence, behaviour and motivation
6 Observed behaviour of children in WEANS	

Area 2:

Measures and indicators of outputs	Measures and indicators of outcomes
Quantitative:	**Quantitative:**
1 Number of volunteers from each ethnic community	1 Number and gravity of racially motivated incidents recorded by police in Weavers End
2 Ethnic background of WEANS committee members and office bearers	2 Levels of participation of different ethnic groups in community events e.g. community conferences
3 Numbers of children from each ethnic community regularly attending WEANS	
Qualitative:	**Qualitative:**
4 Views of volunteers and committee members from different ethnic groups of relationships with others; including acceptance of difference, equality of access to influence and power in WEANS	3 Satisfaction expressed by different ethnic groups about opportunity to express their own culture
5 Degree to which character of activities in WEANS reflects and celebrates ethnic and cultural diversity	4 Satisfaction expressed by different ethnic groups about sense of safety and security
	5 Level of resources invested by community institutions (churches/ mosques/temples, businesses, community organisations) of different ethnic groups in activities contributing to common benefit

In order to use these measures and indicators WEANS realised that they would need to put recording systems in place for their own activities and seek the co-operation of others, particularly the school and police. If they were to see whether WEANS contributed to progress in these areas they would need to know what the situation was now. In other words they had to identify the **baseline** from which they would be evaluating their progress.

As they began to plan **step 7** the WEANS steering group realised that the delivery of the outputs would require them to collect information to help them in future to assess progress and make necessary changes. At first this seemed like a daunting task but four things convinced them that it would be worthwhile:

- They recognised that for reasons such as; health and safety, clarity about decisions and policy, they would have to keep many of the records anyway.
- They recognised that much of the information that they would need would be collected by other people – it was only necessary to get access to the information.
- They were persuaded that they would not know how to improve things if they did not know what they were achieving.
- Very practically, they recognised that if WEANS was to succeed it would need funds to support it – accessing these would be much more likely if it could demonstrate that it was making a real contribution to improvement of the quality of community life.

Moving on to **step 8** the WEANS steering group therefore agreed to collect or request the following data:

1   Number of children of school-age in catchment area; number of children enrolled in WEANS; number actually attending. All information extracted from records.

2   Internal monitoring of time allocated to each activity, and actual participation in each activity through a daily log of activities which would record what activities had been offered and for how long with what number of participants.

3   Minutes and other records of meetings held.

4   Police crime and racial incident records for Weavers End.

5   Overall evidence from the school of relative performance of children attending WEANS.

6   Information arising from the independent health and safety audit.

The steering group also agreed that there would be:

1   Feedback sheets and discussion groups for parents twice a year.

2   Discussion groups with children on a regular basis.

3   Structured interviews once a year with key respondents in the police, the school and social services.

4   Discussion groups of volunteers and committee members once every three months to review progress.

5   An invitation to an impartial observer to visit WEANS at least four times each year.

Using these methods WEANS felt that it would have an on-going process to monitor performance which would enable it to respond to urgent concerns but that it would have a commitment to periodic reviews of progress when the overall change relative to the baseline would be considered. It was agreed that this would be done once per year.

The baseline from which WEANS developed was recorded. First of all, the organisational basis for the development was recorded. WEANS was to be a voluntary project run by a rota of local parents in premises provided by the Catholic church and with equipment purchased from the pump priming grant. It constituted itself from the start as a company limited by guarantee and acquired charitable status. In terms of baseline statistics it was only possible to anticipate the likely level of demand for the service, as this had yet to be tested when WEANS opened for business. But other statistics were available. The group set out what it knew in relation to each of the areas it had decided to focus on:

Area 1: Safe environment and disturbances involving children

1   The primary school role showed that the potential number of children who might use the service was 320.

2   WEANS planned on the basis of the 35 children whose parents had indicated to the steering group that they would be interested in using the service.

3   The primary school league tables of performance had been published for the previous year and there was disappointment that the school had come next to the bottom of the league table for schools in the town in relation to age related test results.

4   The primary school head-teacher reported that there had been an increase of parental complaints about bullying from 7 to 23 in the last year and that these often had a racial dimension to them.

5   Police records showed complaints about vandalism, fighting and shoplifting had each increased between 15 and 30% in the last year.

In relation to area 1, it was noted that until the service was started, satisfaction of parents and children could not be assessed. But during the first year of operation this information would become available as a result of the planned feedback procedures. These would have capacity to show whether views were changing over the year.

Area 2: Relations between ethnic groups

1   Thirty people had volunteered to be involved in WEANS at the recall community conference.

2   Though 40% of the population of the area was black only 8 of the volunteers were from this group. The others were all white.

3   All but five of the volunteers had a close association with the churches, mosque or temple.

4   Minutes of meetings held with the volunteers indicated that there was a concern to get a better balance of volunteers by ethnic background and to widen involvement beyond the faith groups initiating the project.

5   The steering group had agreed that all significant religious and cultural events for all ethnic groups involved in WEANS would be celebrated.

6   Police records showed that there had been 9 serious incidents in Weavers End in the previous year which could be seen as racially motivated.

Another aspect of the baseline was the records of the two community conferences which had led to the setting up of WEANS. Though there was no hard statistical information available about levels of fear and concern about the tensions in the area, there was a strong groundswell of opinion from two well attended events that Weavers End was becoming a less safe and pleasant place to live, especially for members of the ethnic minority communities.

This information was taken as the starting point against which progress could be assessed. Though the date for a periodic review had been set as every 12 months, it soon became apparent that on-going monitoring, evaluation and review was a part of good practice. Very quickly, demand from parents and children exceeded expectations. In the light of records of attendance and early feedback from parents the steering group, supported by the head-teacher, decided after 3 months to apply for funding from the education department to employ a full time co-ordinator. Its application was successful and the programme developed well. Ongoing consultation with children, parents and other stakeholders was informing development. Learning from development, *step 9*, was becoming a feature of normal practice.

Nonetheless, after a year WEANS undertook its first annual review of progress. To do this it reviewed evidence from all sources to compare with the view that had been taken of the baseline position the previous year. The following tables illustrate in summary form the changes identified in relation to each area.

Area 1:

Baseline	Progress year 1
● Number of children who might use the service was 320	● Remains the same
● Scale of planned service 35 (11% of potential users)	● Actually demand for places has risen to 78 (25% of potential users)
● The primary school league table placing 9th of 10	● Age related test performance results for children using WEANS show greater improvement than for other children – League table results place primary school 7th of 10
● Parental complaints about bullying up from 7 to 35 in the last year	● Parental complaints about bullying remain the same but school reports that there are fewer incidents involving children who are attending WEANS
● Police records – complaints about vandalism, fighting and shoplifting up between 15 and 30% in the last year	
● Parents' views of service not yet identified	● Police records show increasing level of complaints
● Children's views of service, and observed behaviour not yet known	● Views of service are generally positive
● Time spent by children in different activities not yet known	● Views of children positive and behaviour and participation positive
● Health and safety to be audited	● More volunteer time than anticipated for homework and arts/drama clubs
	● Audit report satisfactory

Area 2:

Baseline	Progress year 1
• 30 people had volunteered to be involved in WEANS	• 9 volunteers have dropped out but been replaced by 15 new recruits (total 36)
• Though 40% of the population of the area was black only 20% of the volunteers were from this group	• Overall there are now 11 black volunteers (30%)
• All but five of the volunteers had a close association with the churches, mosque or temple.	• Only two of the new volunteers have been attracted through faith groups
• Minutes indicated that there was a concern to get a better balance of volunteers by ethnic background and to widen involvement beyond the faith groups	• There is small improvement in the ratio of black volunteers to population and significant increase in non-faith group related volunteers
• Of 8 WEANS committee members 3 are from the black and ethnic minority communities. None of these are office bearers	• Following annual election number remains three but one is now treasurer of WEANS
• Views of volunteers not yet known	• Black and ethnic minority volunteers less satisfied than white with equal opportunities performance of WEANS
• Views of parents not yet known	• Black and ethnic minority parents less satisfied than white with equal opportunities performance of WEANS
• It was anticipated that 30% of children would be from black and ethnic minority families	• 45% of children attending are from black and ethnic minority families
• All significant religious and cultural events for all ethnic groups to be celebrated	• Sikh, Muslim and Christian festivals have been celebrated but Chinese have not
• Police records showed 9 serious incidents in Weavers End in the previous year which could be seen as racially motivated.	• Number of serious incidents reported to police remains stable
• Strong groundswell of opinion that Weavers End was becoming a less safe and pleasant place to live, especially for members of the ethnic minority communities.	• Children from ethnic minorities express fears to WEANS volunteers. Black parents continue to express concerns but regard WEANS as a symbol of a better future

Though there was much more detailed information available, WEANS management group used this summary as a basis for *step 9* – learning from change. Several important lessons emerged for each area but they realised that there were also outcomes of which they had become aware which they had not anticipated or planned for.

In relation to *Area 1: Safe environment and disturbances involving children*, the key lessons were:

- The outputs that had been planned were not only being delivered but there had also been a major growth in numbers of children participating.

- There appeared to be benefits in terms of the performance of children in the primary school that appeared to have contributed to improved league table standing.

- Bullying remained a problem but WEANS seemed to be having benefits for the children who attended.

- Vandalism was increasing but there was no real evidence about the relationship that WEANS may have had to this.

- Parents were generally satisfied with the service WEANS was providing and increased demand was taken as a broader indicator of satisfaction.

- Children were also positive, more time was being spent in learning related activities than anticipated and this seemed to be connected to the improved performance and behaviour of children in school.

In relation to *Area 2: Relations between ethnic groups*, key lessons were:

- Despite turnover of volunteers the overall number had increased with marginal improvement in participation of black and ethnic minorities and less dependence on faith groups.

- Nonetheless the ratio of black and ethnic minorities volunteers to population remained low.

- Black and ethnic minority involvement of children now exceeded overall population ratio but parents and volunteers from these communities were less satisfied about equal opportunity performance. Not all ethnic or cultural identities were adequately reflected in activities of WEANS.

- Nonetheless WEANS was generally regarded by black and ethnic minority parents and children as a safe and secure setting but the broader environment of Weavers End was still a source of threat. This was reflected in the lack of change in incidents reported to the police.

The following unanticipated outcomes were noted:

- As a result of the increased demand for places WEANS had received a grant from the education department and had become the employer of a co-ordinator. An increased range of responsibilities and skills had been acquired by the committee, however, they were feeling they needed more support than was available to them.

- Evidence of improved performance and behaviour of children in school had led to proposals from the school that WEANS might move from the church hall into spare classroom space in the school. This was met with a mixed response, some committee members and parents felt that it would undermine the independence of WEANS whilst other felt it would offer support.

- The positive development of WEANS had led to publicity in the local press and other communities were seeking advice from WEANS about how to set up a project. WEANS committee were pleased but also felt that this was an increased pressure.

- WEANS had been contacted by the National Association of After-School Care Projects and was beginning to find its advice and networks supportive.

- The Social Services Department had proposed closer links with WEANS. The form that this might take was being discussed but some parents and volunteers were reluctant to have any direct involvement from social workers.

- The Health Promotion Department had heard about the healthy eating project and a health promotion worker had been in touch with WEANS to see if support could be helpful.

Having completed *step 9*, identifying the key lessons from their evaluation, WEANS was now in a position to review its practice and plan for the next stage of its development. WEANS committee members reminded themselves that the ABCD model stressed that community development is a cyclical process – planning, evaluation and learning are continuous activities. They recognised that this meant that they would be continually repeating the steps. Except to bring on board new participants, they did not feel that it was necessary to return to *steps 1–3* which were now well understood, but they would need to:

- go back as for as *step 4* to review whether they had all the necessary stakeholders involved and whether they could improve the participation of some groups – particularly black and ethnic minorities

- revisit *step 5* to renew their vision and define the outcomes which were now most relevant in the light of the lessons from their experience so far

- consider *step 6* to review their vision and outcomes against the dimensions and elements of community development and where necessary identify more suitable indicators and measures of performance

- in the light of their review, implement *steps 7–9* before moving again through the cycle.

One thing that was noticed was that though there was an overall cycle to their planning and evaluation of WEANS, there were also other cycles of planning and evaluation relating to particular parts of its programme. For example, a group of volunteers who were particularly involved in the arts and drama programme decided to use the ABCD principles to look specifically at their activities with the children. Their cycle of review was much shorter but the ABCD process became the basis on which they worked. WEANS encouraged all the projects within WEANS to adopt this approach. The cycle of action, review and change was now established as a feature of the work of WEANS at different levels and in relation to different aspects of its work. Though they often operated in different time scales, the evaluation of the overall WEANS programme could benefit from the evidence that was becoming available within each aspect of its work.

Postscript

WEANS is a hypothetical example but it is based on the experiences of organisations that have used the ABCD model. WEANS' approach to planning and evaluation:

- adapted the model to its own needs
- used straightforward ways of explaining the model
- set realistic and achievable targets
- adopted methods which could be easily integrated into its work
- worked in collaboration with the stakeholders.

These are key messages for any organisation which uses ABCD.